MEXICAN

THE AUSTRALIAN Women's Weekly

contents

snacks and starters   4

meat   26

poultry   46

seafood   62

rice, beans and vegetables   80

salsas   98

sweet treats and drinks   106

glossary   116

index   118

conversion chart   119

Mexican food is perfect fare for the way we live today: not difficult at all to prepare; respendently filled with fresh, healthy ingredients; a very good source of ideas for the vegetarians among us; and equally appealing to children as well as adults, to the adventurous as well as the conservative eater. It's a cuisine deserving of far more attention in our home kitchens.

Pamela Clark
Food Director

pork and cheese quesadillas

preparation time 30 minutes **cooking time** 20 minutes **serves** 4

1 tablespoon olive oil

500g pork mince

1 medium green capsicum (200g), chopped finely

1 fresh long red chilli, chopped finely

1 clove garlic, crushed

½ cup coarsely chopped fresh coriander leaves

8 burrito tortillas

2 tablespoons olive oil, extra

2 cups (250g) coarsely grated cheddar

1   Heat oil in large frying pan; cook mince, stirring, about 10 minutes or until browned. Add capsicum, chilli and garlic; cook, stirring, until fragrant. Remove from heat, stir in coriander.

2   Brush one side of each tortilla with extra oil. Spread pork mixture evenly over half the tortillas, oiled side down; sprinkle with cheese. Top with remaining tortillas, oiled side up.

3   Cook tortillas, in batches, in heated sandwich press or frying pan until browned lightly. Cut quesadillas into quarters; serve with guacamole (see page 102), if desired.

PER SERVING 51.7g fat; 3867kJ (925 cal)

4

SNACKS AND STARTERS

chicken and olive empanadas

preparation time 25 minutes **cooking time** 40 minutes **makes** 24

2 cups (500ml) chicken stock

1 bay leaf

3 chicken thigh fillets (330g)

1 tablespoon olive oil

1 small brown onion (80g), chopped finely

2 cloves garlic, crushed

2 teaspoons ground cumin

½ cup (80g) sultanas

⅓ cup (40g) seeded green olives, chopped coarsely

5 sheets ready-rolled shortcrust pastry

1 egg, beaten lightly

1 Place stock and bay leaf in medium frying pan; bring to a boil. Add chicken, reduce heat; poach chicken, covered, about 10 minutes or until cooked through. Cool chicken in liquid 10 minutes; shred chicken finely. Reserve 1 cup of poaching liquid; discard remainder.

2 Meanwhile, heat oil in large frying pan; cook onion, stirring, until softened. Add garlic and cumin; cook, stirring, until fragrant. Add sultanas and reserved poaching liquid. Bring to a boil then reduce heat; simmer, uncovered, about 15 minutes or until liquid is almost evaporated. Stir in chicken and olives.

3 Preheat oven to moderately hot (200°C/180°C fan-forced). Oil two oven trays.

4 Using 9cm cutter, cut 24 rounds from pastry sheets. Place 1 level tablespoon of the filling in centre of each round; fold round in half to enclose filling, pinching edges to seal. Using tines of fork, press around edges of empanadas to make pattern.

5 Place empanadas on prepared oven trays; brush tops with egg. Bake, uncovered, about 25 minutes or until browned lightly. Serve with yogurt, if desired.

PER EMPANADA 11.6g fat; 840kJ (201 cal)

tortilla lime soup

preparation time 20 minutes **cooking time** 25 minutes **serves** 4

1 medium white onion (150g), chopped coarsely

2 cloves garlic, quartered

1 fresh long red chilli, chopped coarsely

4 medium tomatoes (600g), peeled, quartered

1 tablespoon peanut oil

¼ teaspoon ground allspice

1½ cups (375ml) chicken stock

1.25 litres (5 cups) water

2 teaspoons grated lime rind

¼ cup (60ml) lime juice

¼ cup (70g) tomato paste

⅓ cup (80ml) peanut oil, extra

6 corn tortillas, cut into 2cm-wide strips

1 medium avocado (250g), chopped finely

2 green onions, chopped finely

¼ cup coarsely chopped fresh coriander

1 Blend or process white onion, garlic, chilli and tomato until pureed.

2 Heat oil in large saucepan; cook tomato mixture and allspice, stirring, until fragrant.

3 Add stock, the water, rind, juice and paste. Bring to a boil then reduce heat; simmer, uncovered, about 15 minutes or until mixture thickens.

4 Meanwhile, heat extra oil in medium frying pan; cook tortilla strips in batches, until golden. Drain on absorbent paper. Divide tortilla strips among bowls; ladle soup over. Top with combined avocado, green onion and coriander.

PER SERVING 26g fat; 1777kJ (425 cal)

chipotle beef tostaditas

preparation time 15 minutes (plus standing time) **cooking time** 40 minutes **makes** 36

2 chipotle chillies (10g)

½ cup (125ml) boiling water

12 large white corn tortillas

vegetable oil, for deep-frying

1 tablespoon vegetable oil, extra

1 small brown onion (80g), sliced thinly

1 clove garlic, crushed

300g beef mince

1 tablespoon tomato paste

1 cup (250ml) beer

¼ cup coarsely chopped fresh coriander

½ cup (120g) sour cream

1 Cover chillies with the boiling water in small heatproof bowl; stand 20 minutes.

2 Meanwhile, cut three 7cm-rounds from each tortilla. Heat oil in wok or large frying pan; deep-fry rounds, in batches, until browned lightly. Drain on absorbent paper.

3 Drain chillies over small bowl; reserve liquid. Remove stems from chillies; discard stems. Blend or process chillies and reserved liquid until smooth.

4 Heat extra vegetable oil in medium frying pan; cook onion, stirring, until softened. Add garlic and beef; cook, stirring, until beef is changed in colour. Stir in paste, beer and chilli puree. Bring to a boil then reduce heat; simmer, uncovered, about 15 minutes or until liquid is almost evaporated. Stir in coriander.

5 Top each tortilla crisp with rounded teaspoon of chipotle beef then with ½ teaspoon of sour cream.

PER TOSTADITA 3.2g fat; 238 kJ (57 cal)

chorizo taquitos

preparation time 40 minutes **cooking time** 15 minutes **makes** 40

450g can refried beans

1 tablespoon water

400g chorizo sausage, chopped finely

½ medium red capsicum (100g), chopped finely

3 green onions, chopped finely

10 large flour tortillas, quartered

vegetable oil, for deep-frying

CHUNKY TOMATO SALSA

425g can chopped tomatoes

1 fresh long red chilli, quartered

1 clove garlic, quartered

⅓ cup loosely packed fresh coriander leaves

1 small brown onion (80g), quartered

1 Heat beans with the water in small saucepan.
2 Meanwhile, cook chorizo in large non-stick frying pan, stirring, until crisp; drain on absorbent paper.
3 Combine bean mixture and chorizo in medium bowl with capsicum and onion. Divide filling among tortilla pieces; roll each taquito into cone shape, secure with toothpick.
4 Heat oil in wok or large frying pan; deep-fry taquitos, in batches, until browned lightly. Drain on absorbent paper. Remove toothpicks.
5 Serve hot taquitos with salsa.

CHUNKY TOMATO SALSA Blend or process all ingredients until just combined.

PER TAQUITO 5.2g fat; 337kJ (80 cal)
PER TABLESPOON SALSA 0g fat; 17kJ (4 cal)

bean nachos

preparation time 15 minutes **cooking time** 10 minutes **serves** 4

420g can mexican-style beans, drained

300g can red kidney beans, rinsed, drained, mashed

2 tablespoons tomato paste

1 tablespoon water

230g packet plain corn chips

1½ cups (185g) coarsely grated cheddar

1 large avocado (320g)

1 small red onion (100g), chopped finely

1 large tomato (250g), chopped finely

1 teaspoon lemon juice

½ cup (120g) sour cream

1 tablespoon coarsely chopped fresh coriander

1   Preheat oven to moderately hot (200°C/180°C fan-forced). Heat combined beans, paste and the water, stirring, in large non-stick frying pan. Cover; keep warm.

2   Place corn chips in large ovenproof dish; sprinkle with cheese. Bake about 5 minutes or until cheese melts.

3   Meanwhile, mash avocado in small bowl; stir in half of the combined onion and tomato, and juice.

4   Top heated corn chips with bean mixture, avocado mixture and sour cream; sprinkle nachos with remaining onion and tomato, and coriander.

PER SERVING 60g fat; 3840kJ (917 cal)

crab, prawn and corn cakes

preparation time 20 minutes **cooking time** 35 minutes (plus cooling time) **serves** 4

3 medium potatoes (600g), chopped coarsely

300g can corn kernels, drained

200g cooked medium prawns, chopped coarsely

170g can crab meat, drained

⅓ cup finely chopped fresh coriander leaves

1 egg, beaten lightly

1 tablespoon sweet chilli sauce

½ small red onion (50g), chopped finely

40g butter, melted

1. Boil, steam or microwave potatoes until soft; drain. Mash potatoes until smooth; cool.
2. Preheat oven to hot (220°C/200°C fan-forced).
3. Combine mashed potato, corn, prawns, crab, coriander, egg, sauce and onion in medium bowl.
4. Shape ⅓ cups of mixture into patties; place on oven tray lined with baking paper; brush with butter. Bake 15 minutes; turn carefully, bake a further 15 minutes or until browned lightly. Serve patties with extra sweet chilli sauce, if desired.

PER SERVING 11.1g fat; 1317kJ (315 cal)

deep-fried chimichanga with shredded pork

preparation time 40 minutes **cooking time** 1 hour 10 minutes (plus cooling time) **serves** 8

500g diced pork

2 black peppercorns

3 cloves garlic, peeled

3 cups (750ml) water

1 teaspoon salt

1 teaspoon ground cumin

½ cup chopped fresh coriander

1 small red onion (80g), chopped finely

2 fresh green jalapeño chillies, seeded, chopped finely

8 large flour tortillas

vegetable oil, for deep-frying

1. Combine pork, peppercorns, garlic, the water, salt and cumin in large saucepan; simmer, covered, about 1 hour or until pork is tender; cool in liquid.
2. Drain liquid from pork, discard peppercorns and liquid. Shred pork and garlic, using two forks. Combine pork mixture, coriander, onion and chilli in large bowl.
3. Divide pork mixture evenly between tortillas. Roll tortillas up firmly, secure with toothpick at each end of roll.
4. Heat oil in wok or large frying pan; deep-fry tortilla rolls, in batches, until browned lightly. Drain on absorbent paper.
5. Cut each chimichanga in half on an angle; serve with guacamole (see page 102), if desired.

PER SERVING 14.8g fat; 1279kJ (306 cal)

huevos rancheros

preparation time 10 minutes **cooking time** 30 minutes **serves** 4

1 tablespoon olive oil

1 small red onion (100g), chopped finely

4 medium tomatoes (600g), chopped coarsely

2 tablespoons water

1 tablespoon red wine vinegar

1 medium red capsicum (200g), chopped finely

4 eggs

4 corn tortillas

1 Heat oil in large frying pan; cook onion, stirring, until softened. Add tomato, the water and vinegar. Bring to a boil then reduce heat; simmer, uncovered, 15 minutes, stirring occasionally. Add capsicum; cook, uncovered, 5 minutes.

2 Using large shallow mixing spoon, press four shallow depressions into tomato mixture. Working quickly, break eggs, one at a time, into cup, sliding each egg into one of the hollows in tomato mixture. Cover pan; cook over low heat, about 5 minutes or until eggs are just set.

3 Divide warmed tortillas among plates. Use egg slide to carefully lift egg and tomato mixture onto each tortilla.

PER SERVING 11.2g fat; 1087kJ (206 cal)

black bean soup

preparation time 30 minutes (plus standing time) **cooking time** 2 hours 15 minutes **serves** 8

2½ cups (500g) dried black beans

1kg ham bone

¼ cup (60ml) olive oil

2 medium brown onions (300g), chopped finely

1 medium red capsicum (200g), chopped finely

4 cloves garlic, crushed

1 tablespoon ground cumin

1 teaspoon dried chilli flakes

400g can chopped tomatoes

2.5 litres (10 cups) water

1 tablespoon dried oregano

2 teaspoons ground black pepper

¼ cup (60ml) lime juice

2 medium tomatoes (300g), chopped finely

¼ cup coarsely chopped fresh coriander

1   Place beans in medium bowl, cover with water; stand overnight, drain. Rinse under cold water; drain.

2   Preheat oven to hot (220°C/200°C fan-forced). Roast ham bone on oven tray, uncovered, 30 minutes.

3   Meanwhile, heat oil in large saucepan; cook onion, capsicum and garlic, stirring, about 5 minutes or until vegetables soften. Add cumin and chilli; cook, stirring,1 minute. Add beans and ham bone to pan with undrained tomatoes, the water, oregano and pepper. Bring to a boil then reduce heat; simmer, uncovered, 1½ hours.

4   Remove ham bone from soup; shred ham from bone. Discard bone; add ham to soup, stirring until heated through. Stir juice, tomato and coriander into soup just before serving.

PER SERVING 7.3g fat; 650kJ (155 cal)

roasted tomato and capsicum soup

preparation time 20 minutes **cooking time** 35 minutes **serves** 4

2 large red capsicums (700g)

5 large vine-ripened tomatoes (1.2kg), halved

1 tablespoon olive oil

1 medium brown onion (150g), chopped coarsely

2 cloves garlic, crushed

4 fresh long red chillies, chopped coarsely

2 cups (500ml) water

2 cups (500ml) vegetable stock

cooking-oil spray

2 tablespoons sour cream

2 tablespoons finely chopped fresh chives

1 Preheat oven to very hot (240°C/220°C fan-forced).

2 Quarter capsicums, discard seeds and membranes. Roast capsicum, skin-side up, and tomato, cut-side up, on lightly oiled oven trays, uncovered, about 15 minutes or until capsicum skin blisters and blackens and tomato softens. Cover capsicum pieces with plastic or paper for 5 minutes; peel away skin, cover to keep warm. Cool tomato 5 minutes; peel away skin.

3 Heat oil in large saucepan; cook onion, garlic and chilli, stirring, until onion softens. Add capsicum and tomato; cook, stirring, 5 minutes. Add the water and stock. Bring to a boil then reduce heat; simmer, uncovered, 10 minutes.

4 Blend or process tomato mixture, in batches, until smooth. Pass through fine sieve into large saucepan; discard solids.

5 Divide soup among serving bowls; top with sour cream and chives. Serve with toasted tortilla strips, if desired.

PER SERVING 9.7g fat; 807kJ (193 cal)

polenta carnitas with salsa cruda

preparation time 45 minutes (plus refrigeration time) **cooking time** 1 hour 15 minutes **makes** 40

2 cups (500ml) water

½ cup (125ml) vegetable stock

1 cup (250ml) milk

1½ cups (255g) polenta

20g butter

¾ cup (60g) finely grated parmesan

150g diced pork

½ teaspoon chilli powder

4 black peppercorns

1 clove garlic

1 cup (250ml) water, extra

cooking-oil spray

½ cup (120g) sour cream

SALSA CRUDA

1 medium tomato (190g), seeded, chopped finely

1 small white onion (80g), chopped finely

2 tablespoons finely chopped fresh coriander

2 fresh red thai chillies, seeded, chopped finely

1 tablespoon lime juice

1 Lightly oil 20cm x 30cm lamington pan.
2 Heat the water, stock and milk in large saucepan. Add polenta; cook, stirring, about 5 minutes or until polenta thickens. Stir in butter and cheese. Spoon polenta into prepared pan; press firmly to ensure even thickness. Cool. Cover; refrigerate about 3 hours or until firm.
3 Meanwhile, combine pork, chilli powder, peppercorns, garlic and the extra water in medium saucepan. Bring to a boil then reduce heat; simmer, covered, about 45 minutes or until pork is tender. Cool in liquid.
4 Drain pork, discard peppercorns; shred pork finely.
5 Preheat oven to very hot (240°C/220°C fan-forced). Make salsa cruda.
6 Turn polenta onto board; trim edges. Cut into 3cm x 4cm pieces. Place on oiled oven tray; spray with oil. Bake, uncovered, about 10 minutes or until crisp and browned lightly both sides. Divide salsa cruda, shredded pork and sour cream among polenta pieces.

SALSA CRUDA Combine ingredients in small bowl.

PER CARNITA 2.7g fat; 219kJ (52 cal)
PER TABLESPOON SALSA 0g fat; 10kJ (2 cal)

chile con queso

preparation time 10 minutes **cooking time** 10 minutes **makes** 2 cups

2 teaspoons vegetable oil

½ small green capsicum (75g), chopped finely

½ small brown onion (40g), chopped finely

1 tablespoon pickled jalapeño chillies, chopped finely

1 clove garlic, crushed

½ x 400g can undrained chopped tomatoes

250g cream cheese, softened

1   Heat oil in medium saucepan; cook capsicum, onion, chilli and garlic, stirring, until onion softens. Add tomato; cook, stirring, 2 minutes.
2   Add cheese; whisk until cheese melts and dip is smooth.
3   Serve hot with corn chips, if desired.

PER TABLESPOON 3.9g fat; 174kJ (42 cal)

bean and tomato tostadas

preparation time 10 minutes **cooking time** 10 minutes **makes** 24

1 tablespoon olive oil

1 small brown onion (80g), chopped finely

425g can mexican-style beans, drained

½ cup (130g) bottled tomato salsa

⅓ cup (80g) sour cream

3 large flour tortillas, cut into wedges

½ cup (60g) coarsely grated cheddar

1   Preheat oven to hot (220°C/200°C fan-forced).
2   Heat oil in small frying pan; cook onion, stirring, until softened. Blend or process onion with beans until almost smooth; return to same pan. Add salsa and sour cream; stir until heated through. Place tortilla triangles onto lightly oiled oven trays; top with bean mixture and cheese.
3   Bake tostadas until cheese melts; serve topped with fresh coriander leaves, if desired.

PER TOSTADA 3.4g fat; 259kJ (62 cal)

chilli-poached beef with fresh corn salsa

preparation time 25 minutes **cooking time** 20 minutes **serves** 4

4 chipotle chillies

⅓ cup (80ml) boiling water

1 medium red onion (150g), chopped coarsely

2 cups (500ml) water, extra

1 tablespoon ground cumin

1 cup (250ml) beef stock

300g piece beef eye fillet, cut into 3mm slices

2 tablespoons sour cream

½ cup coarsely chopped fresh coriander

FRESH CORN SALSA

1 medium red onion (150g), chopped coarsely

4 cups (660g) fresh corn kernels

2 cloves garlic, crushed

⅓ cup (80ml) lime juice

3 long green chillies, sliced thinly

1 small avocado (200g), chopped coarsely

1 Soak chillies in the boiling water in small heatproof bowl for 10 minutes. When cool enough to handle, remove stalks from chillies; reserve chillies and liquid.

2 Meanwhile, make fresh corn salsa.

3 Cook onion in lightly oiled large frying pan, stirring, until softened. Add the extra water, cumin, stock, chillies and reserved liquid. Bring to a boil then reduce heat; simmer, uncovered, 10 minutes. Using slotted spoon, remove solids from chilli poaching liquid; reserve.

4 Place beef, in single layer, in chilli poaching liquid; turn off heat. Turn beef over; using slotted spoon, remove beef from liquid after 30 seconds. Cover to keep warm.

5 Blend or process reserved solids with cream until almost smooth. Serve beef on salsa; top with chilli cream sauce and sprinkle with coriander.

FRESH CORN SALSA Combine all ingredients in medium bowl.

PER SERVING 19.8g fat; 1806kJ (432 cal)

MEXICAN

26

beans with spicy sausages

preparation time 20 minutes (plus standing time) **cooking time** 2 hours 15 minutes **serves** 4

1 cup (200g) dried kidney beans

800g spicy beef sausages, chopped coarsely

1 tablespoon olive oil

1 large white onion (200g), chopped coarsely

3 cloves garlic, crushed

1 large red capsicum (350g), chopped coarsely

½ teaspoon ground cumin

2 teaspoons sweet smoked paprika

1 teaspoon dried chilli flakes

2 x 400g cans crushed tomatoes

2 tablespoons coarsely chopped fresh oregano

1 Place beans in medium bowl, cover with cold water; stand overnight, drain. Rinse under cold water; drain. Place beans in medium saucepan of boiling water. Return to a boil then reduce heat; simmer, uncovered, about 30 minutes or until beans are almost tender. Drain.

2 Cook sausages, in batches, in large deep saucepan until browned; drain on absorbent paper.

3 Heat oil in same pan; cook onion, garlic and capsicum, stirring, until onion softens. Add cumin, paprika and chilli; cook, stirring, about 2 minutes or until fragrant. Add beans and undrained tomatoes. Bring to a boil then reduce heat; simmer, covered, about 1 hour or until beans are tender.

4 Return sausages to pan; simmer, covered, about 10 minutes or until sausages are cooked through. Remove from heat; stir in oregano. Serve with flour tortillas, if desired.

PER SERVING 56.9g fat; 3323kJ (795 cal)

MEAT

29

fajitas

preparation time 30 minutes **cooking time** 15 minutes **serves** 4

---

3 cloves garlic, crushed

¼ cup (60ml) lemon juice

2 teaspoons ground cumin

1 tablespoon olive oil

600g beef strips

1 large red capsicum (350g), sliced thickly

1 large green capsicum (350g), sliced thickly

1 medium yellow capsicum (200g), sliced thickly

1 large red onion (300g), sliced thickly

8 large flour tortillas

SALSA CRUDA

2 medium tomatoes (300g), seeded, chopped finely

1 fresh long red chilli, chopped finely

½ cup coarsely chopped fresh coriander

1 clove garlic, crushed

1 small white onion (80g), chopped finely

2 tablespoons lime juice

1 Combine garlic, juice, cumin and oil in large bowl; add beef, stir to coat in mixture. Cover; refrigerate until required.

2 Make salsa cruda.

3 Cook beef, in batches, in heated oiled large frying pan, stirring, until browned all over and cooked as desired. Cover to keep warm. Cook capsicums and onion, in batches, in same pan, stirring, until softened.

4 Meanwhile, heat tortillas according to instructions.

5 Return beef and capsicum mixture to pan; stir gently over medium heat until hot. Divide fajita mixture among serving plates; serve with tortillas and salsa cruda and, if desired, guacamole (see page 102).

SALSA CRUDA Combine ingredients in small bowl.

PER SERVING 20.5g fat; 2646kJ (633 cal)

beef and bean tacos

preparation time 15 minutes **cooking time** 20 minutes **serves** 4

2 cloves garlic, crushed

400g beef mince

1 teaspoon chilli powder

1 teaspoon ground cumin

2 x 300g cans red kidney beans, rinsed, drained

⅓ cup tomato paste

1 cup (250ml) water

2 medium tomatoes (380g), chopped coarsely

8 taco shells

½ small iceberg lettuce, shredded finely

SALSA CRUDA

1 lebanese cucumber (130g), seeded, chopped finely

1 small red onion (80g), chopped finely

2 small tomatoes (260g), seeded, chopped finely

2 teaspoons mild chilli sauce

1 Preheat oven to moderate (180°C/160°C fan-forced).
2 Heat lightly oiled large non-stick frying pan; cook garlic and beef, stirring, until beef is browned all over. Add chilli, cumin, beans, paste, the water and tomato; cook, covered, over low heat about 15 minutes or until mixture thickens slightly.
3 Meanwhile, toast taco shells, upside down and uncovered, on oven tray in oven for 5 minutes.
4 Just before serving, fill shells with beef mixture, lettuce and salsa cruda.

SALSA CRUDA Combine ingredients in small bowl.

PER SERVING 4.9g fat; 723kJ (173 cal)

chipotle pork ribs with chorizo and smoked paprika

preparation time 20 minutes **cooking time** 2 hours 50 minutes **serves** 4

4 chipotle chillies

1 cup (250ml) boiling water

1.5kg pork belly ribs

1 tablespoon olive oil

170g chorizo sausage, sliced thinly

2 medium red onions (340g), chopped coarsely

1 medium red capsicum (200g), chopped coarsely

1 medium green capsicum (200g), chopped coarsely

1 teaspoon smoked paprika

4 cloves garlic, crushed

3 x 400g cans crushed tomatoes

2 medium tomatoes (300g), chopped finely

½ cup finely chopped fresh coriander

2 teaspoons finely grated lime rind

1 clove garlic, crushed, extra

1 Preheat oven to moderately slow (160°C/140°C fan-forced).

2 Soak chillies in the boiling water in small heatproof bowl for 10 minutes. Discard stalks from chillies; reserve chillies and liquid.

3 Using heavy knife, separate ribs. Heat oil in large deep flameproof baking dish; cook ribs, in batches, until browned all over.

4 Cook chorizo, onion, capsicums, paprika and garlic in same dish, stirring, until onion softens. Return ribs to dish with undrained crushed tomatoes, chillies and reserved liquid. Cover; cook in oven about 1 hour. Uncover; cook a further 1½ hours or until ribs are tender.

5 Meanwhile, combine chopped tomato, coriander, rind and extra garlic in small bowl. Cover; refrigerate until required.

6 Top ribs with coriander mixture; serve with chunky corn and zucchini salsa (see page 102) and flour tortillas, if desired.

PER SERVING 90.8g fat; 5003kJ (1197 cal)

barbecued lamb

preparation time 15 minutes (plus refrigeration time) **cooking time** 35 minutes **serves** 8

2kg butterflied leg of lamb

¼ cup (60ml) olive oil

3 cloves garlic, crushed

1 teaspoon ground cumin

1 teaspoon smoked paprika

½ teaspoon brown mustard seeds

1 teaspoon crushed chilli

¾ cup (180ml) dry white wine

1 tablespoon finely chopped fresh rosemary

2 tablespoons brown sugar

1   Place lamb in large shallow dish; pour combined oil, garlic, spices, chilli, wine and rosemary over lamb. Cover; refrigerate 3 hours or overnight.

2   Remove lamb from marinade; place marinade in small saucepan, reserve. Place lamb, covered with foil, on heated oiled grill plate (or grill or barbecue); cook about 30 minutes or until cooked as desired, turning halfway through cooking time.

3   Meanwhile, bring reserved marinade to a boil; reduce heat then simmer, uncovered, 5 minutes..

4   Rub lamb all over with sugar; cook, uncovered, until sugar caramelises. Stand lamb, covered, 10 minutes before slicing.

5   Serve lamb with sauce and a salad of yellow and red teardrop tomatoes, if desired.

PER SERVING 16.9g fat; 1430kJ (342 cal)

MEAT

37

pork and corn tortilla wraps

preparation time 15 minutes **cooking time** 15 minutes **serves** 4

2 tablespoons vegetable oil

½ teaspoon dried oregano

1 teaspoon ground cumin

½ teaspoon chilli powder

600g pork fillet, sliced thinly

16 corn tortillas

310g can corn kernels, drained

3 medium tomatoes (450g), chopped coarsely

1 small red onion (100g), chopped finely

½ cup coarsely chopped fresh coriander

1 butter lettuce, torn

½ cup (120g) sour cream

1 Combine oil, oregano and spices in medium bowl, add pork; toss pork to coat in mixture. Cook pork in heated large non-stick frying pan until cooked as desired.
2 Meanwhile, warm tortillas according to manufacturer's instructions.
3 Combine corn, tomato, onion and coriander in medium bowl.
4 Divide pork, salsa and remaining ingredients among tortillas; roll to enclose filling.

PER SERVING 29.9g fat; 3574kJ (855 cal)

grilled lamb with four-bean salad

preparation time 15 minutes **cooking time** 10 minutes **serves** 4

1 teaspoon sweet paprika

½ teaspoon ground cumin

¼ teaspoon cayenne pepper

800g lamb fillets

1 small red onion (100g), chopped finely

2 small egg tomatoes (260g), chopped coarsely

60g baby spinach leaves, shredded finely

2 x 300g cans four-bean mix, rinsed, drained

¼ cup firmly packed fresh coriander leaves

¼ cup firmly packed fresh flat-leaf parsley

⅓ cup (80ml) bottled vinaigrette

1   Using hands, rub combined spices onto lamb; cook lamb on heated oiled grill plate (or grill or barbecue) until browned and cooked as desired. Cover; stand 5 minutes, slice thickly.

2   Meanwhile, place remaining ingredients in large bowl; toss gently to combine. Serve salad topped with lamb.

PER SERVING 12.5g fat; 1649kJ (394 cal)

beef burritos

preparation time 20 minutes **cooking time** 35 minutes **serves** 4

1 tablespoon olive oil

500g beef mince

1 medium brown onion (150g), chopped finely

1 clove garlic, crushed

1 teaspoon ground cumin

¼ teaspoon chilli powder

400g can crushed tomatoes

½ cup (125ml) water

300g can kidney beans, rinsed, drained

4 large flour tortillas

1 cup (125g) coarsely grated cheddar

1 teaspoon hot paprika

¾ cup (180g) sour cream

1 tablespoon chopped fresh coriander

1 Heat oil in medium frying pan; cook beef, stirring, until browned. Add onion, garlic and spices; cook, stirring, until onion softens. Stir in undrained crushed tomatoes, the water and beans; simmer, uncovered, about 15 minutes or until mixture thickens.

2 Preheat oven to moderately hot (200°C/180°C fan-forced).

3 Divide warm beef filling among tortillas, roll; secure with toothpicks.

4 Place filled tortillas on oiled oven tray; sprinkle with cheese and paprika. Bake about 10 minutes or until heated through. Remove toothpicks; serve topped with sour cream, coriander and, if desired, guacamole (see page 102).

PER SERVING 45.4g fat; 3110kJ (744 cal)

chile con carne

preparation time 10 minutes cooking time 45 minutes serves 4

1 tablespoon olive oil

1 large brown onion (200g), chopped finely

1 clove garlic, crushed

2 fresh long red chillies, chopped finely

500g beef mince

2 x 400g cans chopped tomatoes

⅓ cup (90g) tomato paste

½ teaspoon cayenne pepper

2 teaspoons white sugar

1 cup (250ml) beef stock

420g can red kidney beans, rinsed, drained

1 Heat oil in large saucepan; cook onion, garlic and chilli, stirring, until onion softens. Add mince; cook, stirring, over medium heat until mince is browned lightly.

2 Add undrained tomatoes, paste, pepper, sugar and stock. Bring to boil then reduce heat; simmer, uncovered, stirring occasionally, about 25 minutes or until most of the liquid has evaporated.

3 Add beans; cook, covered, a further 10 minutes. Serve with toasted flour tortillas, if desired.

PER SERVING 14.3g fat; 1576kJ (377 cal)

MEAT

45

chicken quesadillas

preparation time 15 minutes **cooking time** 30 minutes **serves** 4

---

1 tablespoon olive oil

2 cloves garlic, crushed

1 small red onion (100g), chopped finely

¼ teaspoon cayenne pepper

2 teaspoons ground cumin

1 medium red capsicum (200g), chopped finely

1 medium green capsicum (200g), chopped finely

3 cups (480g) shredded barbecued chicken

8 large flour tortillas

2 cups (240g) coarsely grated cheddar

1 Heat oil in large frying pan; cook garlic and onion, stirring, until onion softens. Add spices and capsicums; cook, stirring, until capsicums soften. Remove from heat; stir in chicken.

2 Place one tortilla on board; top with ¼ cup of cheese, then quarter of chicken mixture, then another ¼ cup of cheese. Top with second tortilla. Repeat with remaining tortillas, cheese and chicken mixture.

3 Cook quesadillas, one at a time, uncovered, in same lightly oiled large frying pan, over medium heat, until golden brown. Turn quesadilla, browned-side up, onto large plate then carefully slide back into pan, uncooked-side down. Remove from pan when golden brown both sides; cover to keep warm while cooking remaining quesadillas.

4 Serve quesadillas, cut into quarters, with guacamole (see page 102), dollop of sour cream and shredded iceberg lettuce, if desired.

PER SERVING 40.7g fat; 3352kJ (802 cal)

POULTRY

spicy chicken with black bean and barley salad

preparation time 10 minutes **cooking time** 45 minutes **serves** 4

½ cup (100g) dried black beans

2 cups (500ml) chicken stock

1 litre (4 cups) water

¾ cup (165g) pearl barley

1 teaspoon ground cumin

1 teaspoon smoked paprika

¼ teaspoon chilli powder

¼ cup (60ml) chicken stock, extra

4 chicken breast fillets (680g)

1 large red capsicum (350g), chopped finely

1 clove garlic, crushed

¼ cup (60ml) lime juice

2 teaspoons olive oil

½ cup loosely packed fresh coriander leaves

1   Preheat oven to moderately hot (200°C/180°C fan-forced).

2   Combine beans with half of stock and half of the water in medium saucepan. Bring to a boil then reduce heat; simmer, uncovered, about 45 minutes or until tender, drain. Rinse under cold water; drain.

3   Meanwhile, combine barley with remaining stock and remaining water in medium saucepan. Bring to a boil then reduce heat; simmer, uncovered, until just tender, drain. Rinse under cold water; drain.

4   Combine spices with extra stock in medium bowl, add chicken; toss to coat chicken in mixture. Drain chicken; reserve marinade. Place chicken, in single layer, on metal rack in large shallow baking dish; roast about 30 minutes or until cooked through, brushing with reserved marinade halfway through cooking time. Cover; stand 5 minutes then slice thickly.

5   Place beans and barley in large bowl with remaining ingredients; toss to combine. Divide salad among serving plates; top with chicken.

PER SERVING 8.5g fat; 1826kJ (436 cal)

chicken enchiladas

preparation time 50 minutes (plus standing time) **cooking time** 35 minutes **serves** 10

3 chipotle chillies

1 cup (250ml) boiling water

500g chicken breast fillets

1 tablespoon vegetable oil

1 large red onion (300g), chopped finely

2 cloves garlic, crushed

1 teaspoon ground cumin

1 tablespoon tomato paste

2 x 425g cans crushed tomatoes

1 tablespoon finely chopped fresh oregano

⅔ cup (160g) sour cream

1½ cups (240g) coarsely grated cheddar

10 small flour tortillas

1   Cover chillies with the water in small heatproof bowl; stand 20 minutes. Remove stems from chillies; discard stems. Blend or process chillies with soaking liquid until smooth.

2   Meanwhile, place chicken in medium saucepan of boiling water. Return to a boil then reduce heat; simmer, covered, about 10 minutes or until chicken is cooked through. Remove chicken from poaching liquid; cool 10 minutes. Discard poaching liquid; shred chicken finely.

3   Preheat oven to moderate (180°C/160°C fan-forced). Lightly oil shallow rectangular 3-litre (12-cup) ovenproof dish.

4   Heat oil in large frying pan; cook onion, stirring, until softened. Reserve half of onion in small bowl.

5   Add garlic and cumin to remaining onion in pan; cook, stirring, until fragrant. Add chilli mixture, tomato paste, undrained tomatoes and oregano. Bring to a boil then reduce heat; simmer, uncovered, 1 minute. Remove sauce from heat.

6   Meanwhile, combine shredded chicken, reserved onion, half of sour cream and third of cheese in medium bowl.

7   Heat tortillas according to manufacturer's instructions. Dip tortillas, one at a time, in tomato sauce in pan; place on board. Place ¼ cup of chicken mixture along edge of each tortilla; roll enchiladas to enclose filling.

8   Spread ½ cup tomato sauce into prepared dish. Place enchiladas, seam-side down, in dish (they should fit snugly, without overcrowding). Pour remaining tomato sauce over enchiladas; sprinkle with remaining cheese. Cook, uncovered, about 15 minutes or until cheese melts and enchiladas are heated through. Sprinkle with coriander leaves, if desired. Serve with remaining sour cream.

PER SERVING 9.4g fat; 1593kJ (381 cal)

52

chicken tostadas

preparation time 10 minutes **cooking time** 5 minutes **serves** 4

4 large flour tortillas

½ cup (120g) canned refried beans

½ cup (130g) bottled tomato salsa

3 cups (400g) coarsely chopped cooked chicken

1½ cups (125g) coarsely grated cheddar

4 cups (240g) finely shredded iceberg lettuce

2 medium tomatoes (380g), chopped coarsely

3 green onions, sliced thinly

½ cup (120g) sour cream

1 Preheat grill. Place tortillas, in single layer, on oven trays.

2 Combine beans and salsa in small bowl. Divide bean mixture among tortillas; top with chicken and cheese. Place under preheated grill until cheese melts and tortillas' edges crisp.

3 Serve tostadas topped with lettuce, tomato, onion and sour cream.

PER SERVING 24.5g fat; 1902kJ (455 cal)

grilled chicken with cucumber and tomato salsa

preparation time 10 minutes **cooking time** 15 minutes **serves** 4

4 chicken breast fillets (680g)

2 small tomatoes (260g), seeded, sliced thinly

1 lebanese cucumber (130g), seeded, sliced thinly

1 small red onion (100g), halved, sliced thinly

2 tablespoons sweet chilli sauce

3 teaspoons lime juice

1 tablespoon finely chopped fresh coriander

1 Cook chicken, in batches, on heated oiled grill plate (or grill or barbecue) until browned both sides and cooked through.

2 Meanwhile, combine remaining ingredients in small bowl; toss gently to combine. Serve chicken topped with salsa and grilled lime wedges, if desired.

PER SERVING 9.7g fat; 1099kJ (263 cal)

marinated chilli spatchcock

preparation time 20 minutes (plus refrigeration time) **cooking time** 1 hour **serves** 8

8 fresh long red chillies

8 cloves garlic, peeled

2 small brown onions (200g), chopped coarsely

⅓ cup (80ml) red wine vinegar

1 tablespoon ground cumin

2 tablespoons olive oil

4 medium ripe tomatoes (750g), quartered

4 x 500g spatchcocks

1   Combine chillies, garlic, onion, vinegar and cumin in food processor; blend until almost smooth.

2   Heat oil in frying pan, add onion mixture; cook, stirring, until fragrant.

3   Process tomatoes until smooth. Add to pan with onion mixture; cook, stirring, until mixture boils. Reduce heat; simmer, uncovered, stirring, about 20 minutes or until thickened. Brush spatchcocks with half of chilli sauce; refrigerate 3 hours.

4   Preheat oven to hot (220°C/200°C fan-forced).

5   Place spatchcocks, skin-side up, on rack in shallow baking dish; roast about 30 minutes or until cooked through. Serve spatchcocks with remaining chilli sauce and, if desired, chunky corn and zucchini salsa (see page 102).

PER SERVING 24.5g fat; 1434kJ (343 cal)

paprika chicken with spicy rice

preparation time 10 minutes **cooking time** 20 minutes **serves** 4

½ teaspoon salt

2 teaspoons onion powder

3 teaspoons sweet paprika

1 teaspoon freshly ground black pepper

½ teaspoon chilli powder

1 tablespoon vegetable oil

4 chicken breast fillets (680g)

SPICY RICE

1 tablespoon olive oil

1 medium brown onion (150g), chopped finely

3 garlic cloves, crushed

1 medium green capsicum (200g), chopped finely

1 teaspoon chilli powder

1 teaspoon ground cumin

1 teaspoon ground cinnamon

1 cup (200g) long-grain white rice

2 cups (500ml) water

2 tablespoons lime juice

¼ cup firmly packed, coarsely chopped fresh coriander

310g can corn kernels, rinsed, drained

420g can red kidney beans, rinsed, drained

1 Preheat oven to moderately hot (200°C/180°C fan-forced).

2 Combine salt, spices and oil in medium bowl; coat chicken, one piece at a time, in spice mixture.

3 Place chicken, in single layer, on oiled oven tray; roast about 20 minutes or until chicken is cooked through. Stand 5 minutes; slice thickly.

4 Meanwhile, make spicy rice.

SPICY RICE Heat oil in large saucepan; cook onion and garlic, stirring, until onion softens. Add capsicum and spices; cook, stirring, until fragrant. Add rice; stir to combine then add the water. Bring to a boil then reduce heat; simmer, covered, 15 minutes. Add remaining ingredients; stir until heated through.

PER SERVING 15.3g fat; 2525kJ (604 cal)

chicken and avocado wraps

preparation time 15 minutes **cooking time** 5 minutes **serves** 4

1 large tomato (500g), chopped coarsely

1 medium avocado (500g), chopped coarsely

1 small red onion (100g), chopped coarsely

2 tablespoons coarsely chopped fresh coriander

½ cup (130g) bottled tomato salsa

4 cups (400g) shredded cooked chicken

8 large flour tortillas

TOMATO SALSA

2 medium tomatoes (300g), chopped finely

2 tablespoons pickled jalapeño chillies

¼ cup finely chopped fresh coriander

1 clove garlic, crushed

1 tablespoon lime juice

1   Make tomato salsa.
2   Combine tomato, avocado, onion, coriander, salsa and chicken in large bowl.
3   Warm tortillas according to manufacturer's instructions. Top each tortilla with about an eighth of chicken filling; roll to enclose filling. Repeat with remaining tortillas and chicken filling.

TOMATO SALSA Combine ingredients in medium bowl.

PER SERVING 34.2g fat; 2922kJ (699 cal)

chicken wings with cherry tomato salsa

preparation time 5 minutes (plus refrigeration time) cooking time 25 minutes serves 4

8 large chicken wings (1kg)

½ teaspoon dried oregano

¼ teaspoon chilli powder

1 teaspoon sweet paprika

½ teaspoon ground cumin

2 tablespoons tomato sauce

1 tablespoon vegetable oil

⅓ cup (80ml) lime juice

500g cherry tomatoes

2 medium avocados (500g), chopped coarsely

310g can corn kernels, drained

1 medium red onion (170g), chopped finely

¼ cup firmly packed fresh coriander leaves

1   Preheat oven to moderately hot (200°C/180°C fan-forced).

2   Combine chicken, spices, sauce, oil and 1 tablespoon of juice in large bowl; toss to coat chicken in marinade. Refrigerate 2 hours.

3   Place chicken, in single layer, in oiled large shallow baking dish; roast about 25 minutes or until chicken is cooked through.

4   Meanwhile, quarter tomatoes; combine in medium bowl with avocado, corn, onion, coriander and remaining juice.

5   Serve salsa topped with wings.

PER SERVING 33.5g fat; 2312kJ (553 cal)

fish fillets with grilled corn salad

preparation time 15 minutes **cooking time** 20 minutes **serves** 4

4 x 200g firm white fish fillets

1 tablespoon soy sauce

GRILLED CORN SALAD

2 corn cobs (500g), silk and husks removed

250g cherry tomatoes, halved

1 small red onion (100g), sliced thinly

1 small red thai chilli, seeded, sliced thinly

2 medium avocados (500g), chopped coarsely

¼ cup coarsely chopped fresh coriander

⅓ cup (80ml) lime juice

1 clove garlic, crushed

1 tablespoon olive oil

1   Make grilled corn salad.
2   Brush fish with sauce; cook on heated lightly oiled grill plate (or grill or barbecue) until cooked as desired. Serve fish with salad.
GRILLED CORN SALAD Cook corn on heated oiled grill plate (or grill or barbecue) until browned and just tender; cool 10 minutes. Using sharp knife, remove kernels from cob; combine in medium bowl with remaining ingredients.

PER SERVING 27g fat; 2090kJ (500 cal)

SEAFOOD

char-grilled scallops with corn salsa

preparation time 25 minutes (plus refrigeration time) **cooking time** 20 minutes **serves** 4

32 scallops (800g), roe removed

2 cloves garlic, crushed

2 tablespoons lime juice

1 tablespoon olive oil

2 corn cobs (800g), trimmed

200g grape tomatoes, halved

1 large avocado (320g), chopped coarsely

1 medium red onion (170g), chopped finely

1 medium green capsicum (200g), chopped finely

2 fresh red thai chillies, chopped finely

¼ cup coarsely chopped fresh coriander

8 corn tortillas

LIME DRESSING

2 limes, cut into wedges

¼ cup (60ml) lime juice

½ teaspoon ground cumin

2 teaspoons olive oil

1 Combine scallops, garlic, juice and oil in large bowl. Cover; refrigerate 3 hours or overnight.

2 Make lime dressing.

3 Cook corn on heated oiled grill plate (or grill or barbecue) until browned lightly and just tender. Using sharp knife, cut corn kernels from cobs. Place corn kernels in large bowl with tomato, avocado, onion, capsicum, chilli, coriander and dressing; toss gently to combine.

4 Cook drained scallops, in batches, on same grill plate until browned lightly and cooked as desired. Cover to keep warm.

5 Using tongs, place tortillas, one at a time, briefly, on same grill plate to lightly brown both sides (work quickly as tortillas toughen if overcooked). Wrap tortillas in tea towel to keep warm.

6 Serve scallops with salsa, lime wedges and tortillas.

LIME DRESSING Place ingredients in screw-top jar; shake well to combine.

PER SERVING 25.2g fat; 1204kJ (288 cal)

squid, chorizo and tomato salad

preparation time 30 minutes **cooking time** 15 minutes **serves** 4

900g squid hoods

2 chorizo sausages (340g), sliced thinly

1 tablespoon olive oil

4 medium tomatoes (600g), seeded, sliced thickly

3 x 400g cans white beans, rinsed, drained

2 cups loosely packed fresh flat-leaf parsley leaves

1 teaspoon finely grated lemon rind

¼ cup (60ml) lemon juice

1   Cut squid down centre to open out; score inside in diagonal pattern then cut into 2cm strips.

2   Cook chorizo in heated large non-stick frying pan, stirring occasionally, until browned.

3   Cook squid, in batches, in same reheated pan until tender.

4   Place chorizo and squid in large bowl with remaining ingredients; toss gently to combine.

PER SERVING 29.8g fat; 2519kJ (602 cal)

lime and ginger ceviche

preparation time 20 minutes (plus refrigeration time) **serves** 4

We used kingfish fillets in our recipe, but you can use whatever you prefer – just be certain to buy the freshest sashimi fish you can find because, while the citrus juice changes the colour and texture, the fish in this recipe has not been cooked with heat.

24 scallops (600g), roe removed

400g piece sashimi kingfish, sliced thinly

¼ cup finely grated lime rind

1½ teaspoons sea salt

1 teaspoon cracked black pepper

4 green onions, sliced thinly

2 tablespoons grated fresh ginger

4 lime leaves, shredded finely

1 cup (250ml) lime juice

1   Split scallops in half through centre. Place in large shallow dish with remaining ingredients; toss to coat seafood in marinade. Spread evenly in dish to ensure seafood is submerged in marinade. Cover; refrigerate, stirring occasionally, about 1½ hours or until seafood softens and is almost opaque.

2   Divide ceviche among serving plates; serve with slices of crusty bread and lime wedges, if desired.

PER SERVING 3.2g fat; 744kJ (178 cal)

grilled snapper with spicy tomato and lime sauce

preparation time 15 minutes **cooking time** 15 minutes **serves** 4

2 tablespoons olive oil

3 cloves garlic, crushed

3 green onions (75g), chopped finely

425g can diced tomatoes

1 teaspoon crushed chilli

2 teaspoons white sugar

1 tablespoon lime juice

4 snapper fillets (800g)

75g baby spinach leaves

1   Heat half the oil in small frying pan; cook garlic and onion, stirring, about 1 minute or until onion softens. Stir in undrained tomatoes, chilli, sugar and half the juice. Bring to a boil then reduce heat; simmer, uncovered, about 10 minutes or until liquid has reduced by half.

2   Meanwhile, cook fish in heated lightly oiled large frying pan until cooked as desired.

3   Place spinach in medium bowl with combined remaining juice and oil; toss gently to combine. Serve fish with spicy sauce and spinach salad.

PER SERVING 2.7g fat, 1325kJ (317 cal)

chilli-seared tuna with avocado cream, tortillas and grilled corn

preparation time 30 minutes (plus standing and refrigeration times) **cooking time** 25 minutes **serves** 4

4 chipotle chillies

1 tablespoon olive oil

1 small brown onion (80g), chopped finely

2 cloves garlic, crushed

⅓ cup loosely packed fresh oregano leaves

2 tablespoons tomato paste

2 tablespoons water

4 x 200g tuna steaks

2 trimmed corn cobs (500g)

8 large flour tortillas

2 limes, cut into wedges

AVOCADO CREAM

2 small avocados (400g), chopped coarsely

½ cup (120g) sour cream

¼ cup coarsely chopped fresh coriander leaves

1 tablespoon lime juice

1 Place chillies in small heatproof bowl of boiling water; stand 15 minutes. Drain; chop chillies coarsely.

2 Heat oil in small frying pan; cook onion and garlic, stirring, until onion softens. Stir in chilli, oregano, paste and the water; bring to a boil. Remove from heat; blend or process, pulsing, until mixture forms thick paste.

3 Place fish, in single layer, in large shallow dish; using fingers, pat chilli paste into both sides of fish. Cover; refrigerate 30 minutes.

4 Meanwhile, make avocado cream.

5 Cook corn on heated oiled grill plate (or grill or barbecue) until browned lightly and just tender; slice thickly, cover to keep warm. Cook undrained fish on same heated oiled grill plate until browned both sides and cooked as desired. Cover; stand 5 minutes. Slice fish thickly.

6 Meanwhile, heat tortillas according to manufacturer's instructions. Divide fish, corn, avocado cream and tortillas among serving plates. Serve with lime wedges.

AVOCADO CREAM Blend or process avocado and sour cream until smooth; stir in coriander and juice.

PER SERVING 46.4g fat; 3570kJ (853 cal)

crab and avocado salad

preparation time 20 minutes **cooking time** 5 minutes **serves** 4

250g sugar snap peas, trimmed

1 large apple (200g)

500g cooked blue swimmer crab meat

1 medium red onion (170g), halved, sliced thinly

1 fresh long red chilli, sliced thinly

2 medium avocados (500g), sliced thickly

150g mesclun

¼ cup (60ml) olive oil

¼ cup (60ml) lemon juice

1 clove garlic, crushed

1 Boil, steam or microwave peas until just tender; drain. Rinse under cold water; drain.

2 Slice apple thinly; cut slices into thin strips. Combine peas and apple in large bowl with crab, onion, chilli, avocado and mesclun.

3 Place remaining ingredients in screw-top jar; shake well. Drizzle dressing over salad; toss gently to combine.

PER SERVING 34.5g fat; 1864kJ (446 cal)

slow-cooked spicy garlic prawns

preparation time 20 minutes **cooking time** 30 minutes (plus refrigeration time) **serves** 8

2kg uncooked medium king prawns

4 cloves garlic, crushed

2 fresh long red chillies, chopped coarsely

¾ cup (180ml) olive oil

½ cup (125ml) lemon juice

1 teaspoon sweet paprika

½ cup loosely packed fresh flat-leaf parsley leaves

½ cup loosely packed fresh coriander leaves

¼ cup coarsely chopped fresh chives

1 Preheat oven to slow (150°C/130°C fan-forced).

2 Shell and devein prawns, leaving tails intact.

3 Combine garlic, chilli, oil, juice and paprika in shallow 3-litre (12-cup) baking dish. Add prawns; toss gently to coat prawns in mixture. Cook, covered, about 30 minutes or until prawns are just cooked through; stir once halfway through cooking time. Cover; refrigerate 2 hours.

4 Serve prawns tossed with herbs.

PER SERVING 21.3g fat; 1250kJ (299 cal)

chipotle prawns with grilled pineapple, red onion and coriander salad

preparation time 20 minutes **cooking time** 30 minutes **serves** 4

1kg uncooked medium king prawns

2 medium red onions (340g), cut into wedges

1 small pineapple (800g), chopped coarsely

½ cup firmly packed fresh coriander leaves

CHIPOTLE PASTE

3 chipotle chillies

2 tablespoons apple cider vinegar

2 tablespoons water

1 small brown onion (80g), chopped coarsely

2 cloves garlic, quartered

2 teaspoons ground cumin

1 Make chipotle paste.
2 Shell and devein prawns, leaving tails intact. Combine prawns in medium bowl with half of chipotle paste.
3 Cook onion and pineapple on heated oiled grill plate (or grill or barbecue), uncovered, about 10 minutes or until just tender.
4 Cook prawns on heated oiled grill plate (or grill or barbecue), uncovered, until changed in colour.
5 Combine onion and pineapple in medium bowl with coriander; serve with prawns and remaining chipotle paste.

CHIPOTLE PASTE Soak chillies in vinegar in small bowl for 10 minutes. Blend or process chilli mixture, the water, onion, garlic and cumin until smooth. Place chipotle paste in small saucepan. Bring to a boil then reduce heat; simmer, uncovered, about 10 minutes or until paste thickens.

PER SERVING 1g fat; 773kJ (185 cal)

barbecued corn with chunky salsa and mexican rice

preparation time 20 minutes (plus refrigeration time) **cooking time** 30 minutes **serves** 4

4 untrimmed corn cobs (1.6kg)

2 teaspoons peanut oil

2 cloves garlic, crushed

1 small white onion (80g), chopped finely

1 small red capsicum (150g), chopped finely

1 fresh long red chilli, chopped finely

1½ cups (300g) white medium-grain rice

1 cup (250ml) vegetable stock

1 cup (250ml) water

CHUNKY SALSA

3 medium tomatoes (450g), chopped coarsely

1 small white onion (80g), chopped finely

¼ cup (60g) pickled jalapeño chillies

½ cup coarsely chopped fresh coriander

1 clove garlic, crushed

2 tablespoons lime juice

1 Gently peel husk down corn cob, keeping husk attached at base. Remove as much silk as possible then bring husk back over cob to re-wrap and enclose completely. Place corn in large bowl, add enough cold water to completely submerge corn.

2 Heat oil in medium saucepan; cook garlic, onion, capsicum and chilli, stirring, until onion softens. Add rice; cook, stirring, 1 minute. Add stock and the water. Bring to a boil then reduce heat; simmer, covered, about 20 minutes or until rice is just tender. Remove from heat; fluff rice with fork.

3 Meanwhile, drain corn. Cook corn on heated oiled grill plate (or grill or barbecue) about 25 minutes or until corn is tender, turning occasionally.

4 Make chunky salsa.

5 Serve corn with rice and salsa.

CHUNKY SALSA Combine ingredients for chunky salsa in medium bowl.

PER SERVING 6.7g fat; 2541kJ (608 cal)

RICE, BEANS AND VEGETABLES

banana chillies with potato and green olive stuffing

preparation time 50 minutes **cooking time** 1 hour 10 minutes **serves** 4

40g butter

2 tablespoons olive oil

3 cloves garlic, crushed

2 teaspoons ground cumin

2 teaspoons dried oregano

600g potatoes, diced into 1cm pieces

3 large tomatoes (660g), diced into 1cm pieces

1 cup (120g) seeded green olives, chopped coarsely

2 cups (240g) coarsely grated cheddar

8 red banana chillies (1.3kg)

TOMATO SAUCE

1 tablespoon olive oil

1 clove garlic, crushed

1 medium red onion (170g), chopped coarsely

1 tablespoon ground cumin

2 teaspoons dried oregano

2 x 425g cans diced tomatoes

½ cup (125ml) water

1 Preheat oven to moderate (180°C/160°C fan-forced).

2 Heat butter and oil in large frying pan; cook garlic, cumin, oregano and potato, stirring occasionally, about 10 minutes or until potato browns lightly. Add tomato and olives; cook, stirring, about 10 minutes or until liquid has evaporated. Transfer to large bowl; stir in cheese.

3 Meanwhile, using sharp knife, make small horizontal cut in one chilli 1cm below stem. Make lengthways slit in chilli, starting from horizontal cut and ending 1cm from tip, taking care not to cut all the way through chilli; discard membrane and seeds. Repeat process with remaining chillies. Carefully divide filling among chillies, securing each closed with a toothpick.

4 Make tomato sauce.

5 Place chillies on tomato sauce in dish, cover; cook about 40 minutes or until chillies are tender. Serve chillies with tomato sauce and a mixed green salad, if desired.

TOMATO SAUCE Heat oil in large deep flameproof baking dish; cook garlic, onion, cumin and oregano, stirring, until onion softens. Add undrained tomatoes and the water. Bring to a boil then reduce heat; simmer, uncovered, 10 minutes.

PER SERVING 43.8g fat; 2725 kJ (652 cal)

RICE, BEANS AND VEGETABLES

83

caesar salad

preparation time 30 minutes **cooking time** 20 minutes **serves** 4

Named after Caesar Cardini, the Italian American who tossed the first caesar in his restaurant in Tijuana, Mexico, during the 1920s, this salad must always contain – as authenticated by Cardini's daughter – freshly made garlic croutons, crisp cos lettuce leaves, coddled eggs, lemon juice, olive oil, worcestershire sauce, black pepper and parmesan.

½ loaf crusty bread (220g)

1 clove garlic, crushed

⅓ cup (80ml) olive oil

2 eggs

3 baby cos lettuces (540g), leaves separated

1 cup (80g) flaked parmesan

CAESAR DRESSING

1 clove garlic, crushed

1 tablespoon dijon mustard

2 tablespoons lemon juice

2 teaspoons worcestershire sauce

2 tablespoons olive oil

1   Make caesar dressing.

2   Preheat oven to moderate (180°C/160°C fan-forced).

3   Cut bread into 2cm cubes. Combine garlic and oil in large bowl, add bread; toss bread to coat in oil mixture. Place bread, in single layer, on oven trays; toast in oven about 15 minutes or until croutons are browned lightly.

4   Bring water to a boil in small saucepan; using slotted spoon, carefully lower whole eggs into water. Cover pan tightly, remove from heat; using same slotted spoon, remove eggs from water after 1 minute. When cool enough to handle, break eggs into large bowl, add lettuce; toss gently to combine. Add cheese and croutons.

5   Pour dressing over salad; toss gently to combine. Divide among serving plates; sprinkle with freshly ground black pepper, if desired.

CAESAR DRESSING Place ingredients in screw-top jar; shake well.

PER SERVING 38.4g fat; 2195kJ (525 cal)

warm potato and chorizo salad

preparation time 10 minutes **cooking time** 25 minutes **serves** 4

600g baby new potatoes, halved

3 chorizo sausages (510g), sliced thinly

1 tablespoon olive oil

⅓ cup (80ml) red wine vinegar

2 teaspoons white sugar

1 small red onion (100g), sliced thinly

200g baby spinach leaves

250g cherry tomatoes, halved

1 Boil, steam or microwave potato until just tender; drain.
2 Meanwhile, heat large non-stick frying pan; cook chorizo until crisp, remove from pan.
3 Place potato in same pan; cook, stirring gently, until browned lightly. Remove from pan.
4 Place combined oil, vinegar and sugar in same pan; bring to a boil. Boil, uncovered, about 2 minutes or until dressing reduces slightly.
5 Combine potato and chorizo in large bowl with onion, spinach and tomato; drizzle with dressing.

PER SERVING 33.2g fat; 2086kJ (499 cal)

chilli-glazed sweet potato

preparation time 10 minutes **cooking time** 1 hour **serves** 4

1.5kg kumara, unpeeled

¼ cup (60ml) sweet chilli sauce

1 teaspoon brown mustard seeds

2 tablespoons coarsely chopped fresh rosemary

1 Preheat oven to hot (220°C/200°C fan-forced).

2 Halve kumara lengthways; cut each half into 2cm wedges.

3 Combine remaining ingredients in large bowl, add kumara; toss kumara to coat in mixture. Divide kumara mixture between two large shallow baking dishes. Roast about 1 hour or until kumara is tender and slightly caramelised.

PER SERVING 0.8g fat; 1150kJ (275 cal)

chickpea corn enchiladas

preparation time 25 minutes **cooking time** 15 minutes **serves** 4

1 tablespoon olive oil

1 small white onion (80g), chopped coarsely

1 clove garlic, crushed

1 teaspoon sweet paprika

½ teaspoon ground chilli powder

1 teaspoon ground cumin

400g can tomato puree

300g can chickpeas, rinsed, drained

1 tablespoon coarsely chopped fresh coriander

8 corn tortillas

1 small red onion (100g), chopped coarsely

1 medium tomato (190g), chopped coarsely

1 small avocado (200g), chopped coarsely

½ cup (60g) coarsely grated cheddar

½ cup loosely packed, finely shredded iceberg lettuce

1 Heat oil in medium saucepan; cook onion and garlic, stirring, until onion softens. Add spices; cook, stirring, 2 minutes. Add puree. Bring to a boil then reduce heat; simmer, stirring occasionally, 5 minutes. Add chickpeas and coriander; cook, stirring, until hot.

2 Heat tortillas according to manufacturer's instructions.

3 Divide chickpea mixture and remaining ingredients among tortillas, fold enchiladas to enclose filling.

PER SERVING 19.6g fat; 1434kJ (343 cal)

corn and zucchini fritters with avocado salsa

preparation time 20 minutes **cooking time** 20 minutes **serves** 4

50g butter, melted

½ cup (125ml) milk

¾ cup (110g) plain flour

2 eggs, beaten lightly

210g can creamed corn

2 medium zucchini (240g), grated coarsely

vegetable oil, for shallow-frying

AVOCADO SALSA

3 medium egg tomatoes (225g), chopped coarsely

2 medium avocados (500g), chopped coarsely

1 small red onion (100g), chopped coarsely

2 tablespoons lime juice

2 tablespoons finely chopped fresh coriander

1   Make salsa.
2   Combine butter, milk, flour and egg in medium bowl; whisk until smooth. Add corn and zucchini; mix well.
3   Heat oil in medium frying pan; cook heaped tablespoons of batter about 2 minutes each side or until browned both sides and cooked through. Drain on absorbent paper. Serve warm with salsa.

SALSA Combine ingredients in small bowl.

PER SERVING 54.4g fat; 2700kJ (646 cal)

black bean, corn and chipotle stew

preparation time 15 minutes (plus standing time) **cooking time** 1 hour **serves** 4

1½ cups (300g) dried black beans

2 chipotle chillies

½ cup (125ml) boiling water

1 tablespoon cumin seeds

2 trimmed corn cobs (500g)

2 teaspoons olive oil

1 large brown onion (200g), chopped finely

810g can crushed tomatoes

8 white corn tortillas

SALSA

1 small red onion (100g), chopped coarsely

1 small tomato (90g), chopped coarsely

½ cup coarsely chopped fresh coriander

1 lebanese cucumber (130g), chopped coarsely

1 tablespoon olive oil

2 tablespoons lemon juice

1 Place beans in medium bowl, cover with water; stand overnight, drain. Rinse under cold water; drain. Place beans in medium saucepan of boiling water. Return to a boil then reduce heat; simmer, uncovered, about 15 minutes or until beans are just tender. Drain.

2 Preheat oven to moderately hot (200°C/180°C fan-forced).

3 Place chillies and the boiling water in small bowl; stand 15 minutes. Discard stalks; blend or process chilli and soaking liquid until smooth.

4 Meanwhile, dry-fry cumin seeds in small frying pan, stirring, until fragrant.

5 Cook corn on heated oiled grill plate (or grill or barbecue) until browned lightly and just tender. When cool enough to handle, cut kernels from cobs with sharp knife.

6 Heat oil in large flameproof dish; cook onion, stirring, until softened. Add drained beans, chilli mixture, cumin, undrained tomatoes and half of corn; bring to a boil. Cook in oven about 20 minutes or until sauce thickens.

7 Meanwhile, heat tortillas according to manufacturer's instructions. Make salsa.

8 Serve stew with tortillas and salsa.

SALSA Combine remaining corn with salsa ingredients in medium bowl.

PER SERVING 10.4g fat; 1839kJ (440 cal)

bean salad with tortilla chips

preparation time 20 minutes **cooking time** 5 minutes **serves** 4

4 medium tomatoes (600g), seeded, chopped coarsely

420g can four-bean mix, rinsed, drained

300g can kidney beans, rinsed, drained

½ cup coarsely chopped fresh coriander

¼ cup (60ml) lime juice

1 small red onion (100g), chopped finely

2 fresh long red chillies, chopped finely

4 small flour tortillas, cut into wedges

1 small avocado (200g)

2 tablespoons sour cream

1 Preheat oven to moderately hot (200°C/180°C fan-forced).

2 Combine tomato, beans, half of coriander, 1 tablespoon of juice, half of onion and half of chilli in medium bowl.

3 Place tortilla wedges, in single layer, on oven tray; toast about 5 minutes or until crisp.

4 Meanwhile, mash avocado in small bowl; stir in remaining coriander, juice, onion and chilli.

5 Divide tortilla chips among plates; top with bean mixture, guacamole and sour cream.

PER SERVING 16g fat; 1726kJ (413 cal)

drunken beans

preparation time 10 minutes (plus standing time) **cooking time** 1 hour 40 minutes **serves** 4

1 cup (200g) dried pinto beans

3 bacon rashers (210g), rind removed, chopped coarsely

1 medium brown onion (150g), chopped finely

1 clove garlic, crushed

1 teaspoon ground cumin

½ teaspoon cayenne pepper

1 tablespoon tomato paste

425g can crushed tomatoes

1 cup (250ml) water

1 cup (250ml) beer

1 tablespoon worcestershire sauce

2 tablespoons brown sugar

1   Place beans in medium bowl, cover with water; stand overnight. Drain.

2   Cook bacon, onion, garlic and spices in lightly oiled large saucepan, stirring, until onion softens. Add drained beans and remaining ingredients. Bring to a boil then reduce heat; simmer, covered, about 1½ hours or until beans are just tender.

PER SERVING 5.1g fat; 1196kJ (286 cal)

salsa fresca

preparation time 20 minutes **makes** 1 cup

½ cup finely chopped fresh flat-leaf parsley

¼ cup finely chopped fresh dill

¼ cup finely chopped fresh chives

1 tablespoon wholegrain mustard

2 tablespoons lemon juice

2 tablespoons drained, rinsed baby capers, chopped finely

1 clove garlic, crushed

⅓ cup (80ml) olive oil

1   Combine ingredients in small bowl.

TIP Goes well with grilled lamb; pork chops.

PER TABLESPOON 6.1g fat; 242kJ (58 cal)

mango and avocado salsa

preparation time 15 minutes **makes** 2½ cups

1 medium mango (430g), chopped coarsely

1 large avocado (320g), chopped coarsely

1 small red onion (100g), chopped finely

1 small red capsicum (150g), chopped finely

1 fresh small red chilli, chopped finely

2 tablespoons lime juice

1   Combine ingredients in medium bowl.

TIP Goes well with roasted sweet corn, red onion and black bean salad; grilled salmon fillets.

PER TABLESPOON 1.7g fat; 100kJ (24 cal)

SALSAS

black bean salsa

preparation time 15 minutes (plus standing time) **cooking time** 20 minutes **makes** 4 cups

¾ cup (150g) dried black beans, cooked

2 medium red capsicums (400g), roasted, peeled, sliced thinly

2 cups frozen corn kernels

1 small red onion (100g), chopped finely

1 fresh long red chilli, chopped finely

⅓ cup coarsely chopped fresh coriander

2 cloves garlic, crushed

2 tablespoons olive oil

1 tablespoon finely grated lime rind

½ cup (125ml) lime juice

1 teaspoon ground cumin

1   Place beans in small bowl, cover with water; stand overnight. Drain.

2   Place beans in medium saucepan of boiling water. Return to a boil, then reduce heat; simmer, uncovered, about 15 minutes or until beans are just tender. Drain.

3   Combine beans with remaining ingredients in large bowl.

TIP   Goes well with grilled lamb chops; chicken and cheese tostadas.

PER TABLESPOON   0.9g fat; 109kJ (26 cal)

char-grilled capsicum and green olive salsa

preparation time 15 minutes **cooking time** 10 minutes **makes** 2 cups

2 cups (240g) seeded green olives, chopped coarsely

150g char-grilled red capsicum, drained

1 small red onion (100g), chopped finely

1 tablespoon lime juice

⅓ cup coarsely chopped fresh coriander

1   Blend or process half of olives until smooth. Transfer to medium bowl; stir in capsicum, remaining olives, onion, juice and coriander.

TIP   Goes well with grilled lamb fillets; as a dip with warm tortillas; or on an antipasti platter.

PER TABLESPOON   0.1g fat; 59kJ (14 cal)

chunky corn and zucchini salsa

preparation time 20 minutes **cooking time** 10 minutes **makes** 7 cups

2 corn cobs (800g), trimmed

100g baby zucchini, halved lengthways

2 large avocados (640g), chopped coarsely

200g grape tomatoes, halved

1 medium red onion (170g), sliced thickly

¼ cup coarsely chopped fresh coriander

1 tablespoon sweet chilli sauce

⅓ cup (80ml) lime juice

2 fresh small red chillies, sliced thinly

1   Cook corn and zucchini on heated oiled grill plate (or grill or barbecue) until tender and browned lightly. Using sharp knife, remove kernels from cobs.

2   Combine corn and zucchini in large bowl with avocado, tomato, onion and coriander. Add remaining ingredients; toss gently to combine.

TIP   Goes well with pork ribs and marinated spatchcock.

PER TABLESPOON 1.3g fat; 84kJ (20 cal)

guacamole

preparation time 10 minutes **makes** 2½ cups

2 medium avocados (500g)

½ small red onion (50g), chopped finely

1 medium egg tomato (75g), seeded, chopped finely

1 tablespoon lime juice

¼ cup coarsely chopped fresh coriander

1   Mash avocados in medium bowl; stir in remaining ingredients.

TIP   Goes well with nachos, burritos and fajitas.

PER TABLESPOON 4g fat; 157kJ (38 cal)

corn and tomato relish

preparation time 15 minutes **cooking time** 1 hour 30 minutes **makes** 4 cups

2 x 400g cans diced tomatoes

1 medium red capsicum (200g), chopped finely

1 large brown onion (200g), sliced thinly

1 teaspoon salt

1 cup (220g) white sugar

1 cup (250ml) white wine vinegar

1½ tablespoons mustard powder

420g can corn kernels, drained

2 tablespoons cornflour

1 tablespoon water

1 Combine undrained tomatoes, capsicum, onion, salt, sugar, vinegar and mustard powder in medium pan. Bring to a boil then reduce heat; simmer, uncovered, 1 hour, stirring occasionally. Add corn; simmer, uncovered, a further 20 minutes.

2 Blend cornflour and the water in small bowl to form a smooth paste; stir into corn mixture. Bring to a boil then reduce heat; simmer, uncovered, about 5 minutes or until thickened slightly.

3 Transfer mixture to hot, sterilised jars; seal. Allow to cool, then refrigerate until required.

TIP Goes well with cold meats.

PER TABLESPOON 0.1g fat; 134kJ (32 cal)

tomato and chilli and raisin relish

preparation time 15 minutes **cooking time** 1 hour 10 minutes **makes** 2 cups

4 large tomatoes (880g), peeled, chopped coarsely

1 medium brown onion (150g), chopped coarsely

½ cup (110g) firmly packed brown sugar

1 cup (250ml) white wine vinegar

1 tablespoon ground ginger

1 medium green apple (150g), chopped coarsely

½ cup (85g) raisins

1 teaspoon dried chilli flakes

1 teaspoon cracked black pepper

2 tablespoons tomato paste

1 Combine ingredients in large saucepan; bring to a boil, stirring. Reduce heat; simmer, uncovered, stirring occasionally, about 1 hour or until relish thickens.

2 Transfer mixture to hot, sterilised jars; seal. Allow to cool, then refrigerate until required.

TIP Goes well with grilled lamb chops; corn chips.

PER ¼-CUP SERVING 0.2g fat; 481kJ (115 cal)

caramel flans

preparation time 25 minutes (plus refrigeration time) **cooking time** 55 minutes **makes** 6

¾ cup (165g) caster sugar

¾ cup (180ml) water

3 eggs

3 egg yolks

½ cup (110g) caster sugar, extra

1 cup (250ml) milk

1½ cups (375ml) cream

1   Preheat oven to slow (150°C/130°C fan-forced).

2   Combine sugar and the water in medium saucepan; stir over low heat, without boiling, until sugar dissolves. Brush down side of pan with pastry brush dipped in water to remove any sugar grains. Bring to a boil; boil, uncovered, without stirring, until mixture is caramel in colour. Remove from heat; divide between six ¾-cup (180ml) ovenproof moulds.

3   Whisk eggs, yolks and extra sugar in medium bowl until just combined. Bring milk and cream to a boil in small saucepan; gradually whisk into egg mixture until combined. Strain mixture into large jug.

4   Pour custard over toffee in moulds; place moulds into baking dish. Pour enough boiling water into baking dish to come three-quarters of the way up side of moulds.

5   Bake about 35 minutes or until flans are just set. Remove from baking dish; refrigerate overnight.

6   Gently pull flans away from side of moulds. Invert onto serving plates.

PER FLAN 34.1g fat; 2182kJ (522 cal)

SWEET TREATS AND DRINKS

rice pudding with dried fruit compote

preparation time 20 minutes (plus standing time) **cooking time** 1 hour 5 minutes **serves** 4

1 litre (4 cups) milk

⅓ cup (75g) caster sugar

10cm strip lemon rind

⅓ cup (65g) white medium-grain rice

2 teaspoons cornflour

1 tablespoon water

2 egg yolks

½ teaspoon vanilla extract

DRIED FRUIT COMPOTE

½ cup (75g) coarsely chopped dried pear

½ cup (45g) coarsely chopped dried apple

½ cup (85g) coarsely chopped seeded prunes

2 cups (500ml) water

2 tablespoons honey

1 cinnamon stick

1 Combine milk in medium saucepan with sugar and rind; bring to a boil, stirring occasionally. Gradually stir in rice, reduce heat; simmer, covered, about 40 minutes or until rice is tender, stirring occasionally. Discard rind.

2 Meanwhile, make dried fruit compote.

3 Blend cornflour with the water in small bowl; stir in yolks. Stir in heaped tablespoon of hot creamed rice; pour egg mixture into creamed rice. Stir over medium heat until mixture boils and thickens. Stir in extract; remove from heat. Stand 15 minutes before serving with compote.

DRIED FRUIT COMPOTE Place ingredients in medium saucepan. Bring to a boil then reduce heat; simmer, uncovered, 15 minutes. Remove from heat; discard cinnamon stick.

PER SERVING 12.9g fat; 2082kJ (498 cal)

wedding cookies

preparation time 30 minutes (plus refrigeration time) **cooking time** 25 minutes **makes** 40

250g butter, softened

¾ cup (160g) caster sugar

2 cups (300g) plain flour

½ cup (80g) finely chopped blanched almonds

½ cup (60g) finely chopped pecans

1 tablespoon finely grated orange rind

1 teaspoon vanilla extract

1 egg yolk

¼ cup (40g) icing sugar mixture

1 Preheat oven to moderate (180°C/160°C fan-forced).

2 Beat butter and sugar in small bowl with electric mixer until light and fluffy. Stir in sifted flour, nuts, rind, extract and yolk.

3 Shape level tablespoons of dough into rectangles; place on oven trays lined with baking paper. Cover; refrigerate 30 minutes. Bake about 25 minutes or until lightly browned. Cool on wire racks, dust with sifted icing sugar mixture.

PER COOKIE 7.5g fat; 477kJ (114 cal)

grilled mango cheeks

preparation time 10 minutes **cooking time** 5 minutes **serves** 4

4 small mangoes (1.2kg)

2 tablespoons brown sugar

1 litre mango sorbet

1 lime, cut into wedges

1   Preheat grill.

2   Cut down both sides of mango seed to remove cheeks. Score mango flesh at 1.5cm intervals then score again in opposite direction to create diamond pattern.

3   Sprinkle 1 teaspoon of sugar on surface of each mango half; grill about 5 minutes or until browned lightly.

4   Serve mangoes with sorbet and lime wedges.

PER SERVING 0.5g fat; 1718kJ (411 cal)

coconut ice-cream

preparation time 15 minutes (plus refrigeration time) **cooking time** 10 minutes **serves** 6

400ml can coconut cream

300ml cream

1 cup (250ml) milk

1 vanilla bean

6 egg yolks

¾ cup (165g) caster sugar

⅔ cup (60g) desiccated coconut

1   Combine coconut cream, cream and milk in small saucepan. Split vanilla bean in half lengthways; scrape seeds into pan then place pod in pan. Bring cream mixture to a boil; strain into large heatproof jug, discard pod.

2   Whisk yolks and sugar in medium bowl until just combined; gradually whisk in hot cream mixture. Strain mixture into large jug.

3   Return mixture to same pan; stir over low heat, without boiling, until mixture is thickened slightly; stir in coconut. Pour mixture into lamington pan, cover; freeze until almost set.

4   Chop ice-cream roughly, beat in large bowl with electric mixer, or process, until smooth. Pour into loaf pan, cover; freeze until firm.

TIP   Ice-cream can be made in ice-cream machine, following manufacturer's instructions.

PER SERVING 49.2g fat; 2508kJ (600 cal)

hot chocolate

preparation time 5 minutes **cooking time** 5 minutes **serves** 6

1 litre (4 cups) milk

250g mexican chocolate, chopped

¾ cup (180ml) thickened cream

1   Combine milk and chocolate in medium saucepan; stir over low heat until chocolate is melted. Do not boil.

2   Beat cream in small bowl with electric mixer until soft peaks form.

3   Divide chocolate mixture among heatproof serving glasses, top with whipped cream.

TIP Mexican chocolate can be replaced with 250g dark eating chocolate and 1 teaspoon ground cinnamon.

PER SERVING 29.6g fat; 1802kJ (431 cal)

lime and mint cooler

preparation time 10 minutes (plus refrigeration time) **cooking time** 5 minutes **serves** 4

1 cup (250ml) lime juice

1.25 litres (5 cups) chilled mineral water

¼ cup coarsely chopped fresh mint

SUGAR SYRUP

½ cup (125ml) water

½ cup (110g) caster sugar

1   Make sugar syrup.

2   Combine syrup in large jug with juice, mineral water and mint. Serve immediately, with ice if desired.

SUGAR SYRUP Combine ingredients in small saucepan; stir over heat until sugar dissolves. Bring to a boil, remove from heat; refrigerate until cold.

PER CUP 0.1g fat; 252kJ (60 cal)

classic margarita

preparation time 5 minutes **serves** 1

45ml dark tequila

30ml Cointreau

30ml lime juice

30ml sugar syrup*

1 cup ice cubes

salt

1 lime, sliced

1   Combine tequila, cointreau, juice, syrup and ice in cocktail shaker; shake vigorously. Rub lime slice around rim of 150ml margarita glass; turn glass upside-down and dip wet rim into saucer of salt. Strain margarita into salt-rimmed glass. Garnish with lime slice.

PER CUP 0.3g fat; 4360kJ (1043 cal)

*sugar syrup

Stir 1 cup (220g) caster sugar with 1 cup (250ml) water in small saucepan, over low heat, until sugar dissolves. Bring to a boil then reduce heat; simmer, uncovered, without stirring, 5 minutes. Remove from heat; cool to room temperature.

TIP Sugar syrup can be stored in refrigerator for up to three weeks.

blood orange margarita

preparation time 5 minutes **serves** 1

45ml dark tequila

30ml lime juice

30ml blood orange juice

30ml sugar syrup*

1 cup ice cubes

1   Combine ingredients in cocktail shaker; shake vigorously. Strain into salt-rimmed 150ml margarita glass (see previous recipe). Garnish with blood orange slice, if desired.

PER CUP 0.1g fat; 1296kJ (310 cal)

chilli margarita

preparation time 5 minutes **serves** 1

20ml dark tequila

10ml Cointreau

30ml sugar syrup*

10ml lime juice

1 red thai chilli, chopped finely

dash Tabasco sauce

1 cup ice cubes

1   Combine ingredients in cocktail shaker; shake vigorously. Strain into 150ml margarita glass. Garnish with lime slice and fresh red chilli, if desired.

PER CUP 0.1g fat; 3720kJ (890 cal)

sangria mexicana

preparation time 15 minutes **serves** 4

750ml bottle dry red wine

30ml Cointreau

30ml Bacardi

30ml brandy

½ cup (110g) white sugar

2 cinnamon sticks

½ medium orange, peeled, chopped coarsely

1 medium lime, peeled, chopped coarsely

6 medium strawberries, chopped coarsely

1 cup ice cubes

1   Place ingredients in large jug; stir until well combined; pour into highball glasses.

PER CUP 0.1g fat; 1304kJ (312 cal)

BEANS

black an earthy-flavoured dried bean; also known as turtle beans or black kidney beans.

black-eyed also known as black-eyed peas, are the dried seed of a variant of the snake or yard bean.

borlotti also known as roman beans, they can be eaten fresh or dried. Are a pale pink or beige colour with darker red spots.

kidney medium-size red bean, slightly floury in texture yet sweet in flavour; sold dried or canned, it is found in bean mixes and is used in chile con carne.

lima large, flat, kidney-shaped, beige, dried and canned bean. Also known as butter beans.

pinto similar to borlotti, a plump, kidney-shaped, pinky beige bean speckled with brown to red streaks; available canned or dried.

refried pinto or borlotti beans, cooked twice—soaked and boiled, then mashed and fried, traditionally in lard. A Mexican staple, frijoles refritos (refried beans) are available canned.

sprouts also known as bean shoots; tender new growths of assorted beans and seeds germinated for consumption as sprouts.

white in this book, some of the recipes call for 'white beans'; this is a generic term that we use for canned or dried navy, cannellini, haricot or great northern beans.

BEEF

chuck inexpensive cut from the neck and shoulder area.

eye-fillet most expensive cut; a fine cut that is extremely tender.

gravy boneless stewing beef cut from the shin; slow-cooked, it imbues stocks and casseroles with a gelatine richness.

minced also known as ground beef. Chuck steak is often used.

new york cut striploin steak with no bone.

round steak boneless cut from the tender muscle running from rump to ankle; used in stir-fries, minute steaks and schnitzel.

skirt steak lean, flavourful coarse-grained cut from the inner thigh. Needs slow cooking; good for stews or casseroles.

BEETROOT also known as red beets; a round root vegetable.

BLOOD ORANGE a virtually seedless citrus fruit with blood-red streaked rind and flesh; has sweet, non-acidic, salmon-coloured pulp and juice. It is thought to have occurred in nature by accident in 17th-century Sicily. The juice can be drunk straight or may be used in cocktails, sauces and jellies. The rind is not as bitter as that of an ordinary orange.

BREADS

ciabatta in Italian, the word means slipper, which is the traditional shape of this popular crisp-crusted white bread.

pitta also known as lebanese bread. Is sold in large, flat pieces that separate into two thin rounds. Also available in small thick pieces called pocket pitta.

sourdough so-named, not because it's sour in taste, but because it is made by using a small amount of 'starter dough', which contains a yeast culture, mixed into flour and water. Part of the resulting dough is then saved to use as starter dough next time.

tortilla thin, round unleavened bread originating in Mexico. Made from either wheat flour or corn. Can be fried to make crisp taco shells, stuffed with beans, sour cream and cheese and baked (enchiladas), torn into strips and fried to make scoops for salsas (tostaditas), or fried and stacked one on top of the other with a filling placed between each one (tostadas).

BURRITO a dish comprised of wheat flour tortillas wrapped to encase shredded meat, beans and cheese. The ends are turned in to contain the filling.

CAPSICUM also known as bell pepper or pepper. Discard seeds and membranes before use.

CARDAMOM native to India; can be purchased in pod, seed or ground form. Has a distinctive aromatic, sweetly rich flavour, and is one of the world's most expensive spices.

CHEESE

fetta crumbly goat- or sheep-milk cheese with salty taste.

haloumi a firm, cream-coloured sheep-milk cheese; somewhat like a minty, salty fetta in flavour. Can be grilled or fried, briefly, without breaking down.

manchego named for the Spanish region of La Mancha where it is produced. Made from pasturised sheep's milk. The grey or buff-coloured rind is marked with a crosshatch pattern; the interior ranges from bright to white to pale yellow, depending on the age of the cheese. Has a number of holes and a mild, slightly briny, nutty flavour. The final cheese is usually smeared with olive oil.

mozzarella soft, spun-curd cheese traditionally made from water-buffalo milk.

ricotta soft, white, cow-milk cheese. Is a sweet, moist cheese with a slightly grainy texture and a fat content of around 8.5%.

romano a hard cheese made from cow or sheep milk. Straw-coloured and grainy in texture, it is mainly used for grating. Parmesan can be substituted.

parmesan also known as parmigiano, parmesan is a hard, grainy cow-milk cheese.

CHICKPEAS also called channa, garbanzos or hummus; a sandy-coloured, irregularly round, legume, often used in Hispanic and Mediterranean cooking. Firm texture, even after cooking, and a floury consistency with a robust, nutty flavour; available canned or dried (the latter need several hours reconstituting in cold water before being used).

CHILLI

cayenne pepper a thin-fleshed, long, extremely hot, dried red chilli, usually purchased ground; both arbol and guajillo chillies are the fresh sources for cayenne.

chipotle chillies also known as ahumado chillies, they are dried, smoked jalapeños. They have a deeply intense smoky flavour rather than a blast of heat. They average 6cm in length and are dark brown, almost black.

green any unripened chilli; also some particular varieties that are ripe when green, such as jalapeño, habanero, poblano or serrano.

flakes, dried deep-red dehydrated very fine slices and whole seeds; good for cooking or for sprinkling over already-cooked food.

jalapeños pronounced hah-lah-pain-yo. Fairly hot, green chillies, available bottled in brine or fresh from greengrocers.

thai red small, medium hot, and bright red in colour.

CHIMICHANGA a deep-fried burrito.

CHORIZO sausage of Spanish origin, made of coarsely ground pork and highly seasoned with garlic and chilli.

COOKING-OIL SPRAY we used a cholesterol-free cooking spray made from canola oil.

CINNAMON available both in the piece (called sticks or quills) and ground into a powder. One of the world's most common spices, used universally as a sweet, fragrant flavouring for

GLOSSARY

both sweet and savoury foods. The dried inner bark of the shoots of the Sri Lankan native cinnamon tree; much of what is sold as the real thing is, in fact, cassia, Chinese cinnamon, from the bark of the cassia tree. Less expensive to process than true cinnamon, it is blended with Sri Lankan cinnamon to make the type of 'cinnamon' commonly found in supermarkets.

COCONUT
cream in cans and cartons; made from coconut and water.
milk not the juice inside the fruit, which is known as coconut water, but the diluted liquid that comes from the second pressing of the white meat of a mature coconut. Coconut cream comes from the first pressing.

CORIANDER also known as cilantro or chinese parsley; this bright-green-leafed herb has a pungent flavour. Both stems and roots are used in Thai cooking.

CRAB
blue swimmer also known as blue crab and sand crab. Has a soft, sweet flesh; sold whole or as crab meat. Steam, poach, bake, stir-fry, grill or barbecue.
mud also known as green crab, black crab, mangrove. Moist, sweet, flaky flesh. Cook as above.

CUMIN also known as zeera; related to the parsley family. Has a spicy, nutty flavour. Available in seed form or dried and ground.

CURLY ENDIVE also known as frisee, a curly-leafed green vegetable, mainly used in salads.

EGGPLANT also known as aubergine; ranging in size from tiny to very large and in colour from pale green to deep purple, eggplant has an equally wide variety of flavours.

ENCHILADAS baked tortillas stuffed with beans, cheese and sour cream.

FENNEL also known as anise or finocchio; can be eaten raw or braised or fried. Also the name given to dried seeds having a licorice flavour.

FRITTATA a egg dish similar to an omelette; the filling of meat, vegetables, seafood or various other ingredients is stirred into the uncooked egg mixture, rather than being added once the eggs are nearly cooked.

GINGER
fresh also known as green or root ginger; the thick gnarled root of a tropical plant.
ground also known as powdered ginger; cannot be substituted for fresh ginger.
pickled pink pickled paper-thin shavings of ginger in a mixture of vinegar, sugar and natural colouring. Available, packaged, from Asian grocery stores.

HAM HOCK is the lower portion of a hog's hind leg. It consists of bone, flesh, fat and connective tissue. Usually smoked or cured, but also fresh, ham hocks are mainly used to flavour soups.

HUEVOS RANCHEROS an egg dish served for breakfast; eggs and tomato salsa on tortillas.

LAMB
backstrap also known as eye of loin; the larger fillet from a row of loin chops or cutlets. Tender, best cooked rapidly; barbecued or pan-fried.
chump cut from above the hind legs to the mid-loin section; can be used as a piece for roasting or cut into chops.

LEBANESE CUCUMBER short, slender and thin-skinned; also known as european or burpless cucumber.

LEMON GRASS a tall, clumping, sharp-edged grass that smells and tastes of lemons; the lower part of the stem is chopped and used in Asian cooking or for tea.

MESCLUN a salad mixture of assorted young lettuce and other green leaves; sometimes also contains edible flowers.

MUSHROOMS
flat large, flat mushrooms with a rich earthy flavour, they are ideal for filling and barbecuing. Sometimes misnamed field mushrooms, which are, in fact, wild mushrooms.
oyster also known as abalone; grey-white mushroom shaped like a fan. Has a smooth texture and subtle, oyster-like flavour.
shiitake when fresh are also known as chinese black, forest or golden oak mushrooms; are large and meaty and have the earthiness and taste of wild mushrooms. When dried, they are known as donko or dried chinese mushrooms; rehydrate before use.
swiss brown light to dark brown mushrooms with full-bodied flavour.

MUSTARD
mustard seeds black, known as brown mustard seeds, are more pungent than the white variety; used frequently in curries. White, also know as yellow mustard seeds are ground for mustard powder and for use in prepared mustards.
wholegrain also known as seeded. A French-style coarse-grain mustard made from crushed mustard seeds and dijon-style french mustard.

NUTMEG the dried nut of a tropical tree; available in ground form, or you can grate your own with a fine grater.

ONIONS
green also known as scallion or, incorrectly, shallot; an immature onion picked before the bulb has formed, with a long, bright-green edible stalk.
red also known as spanish, red spanish or bermuda onion;

a sweet-flavoured, large, purple-red onion.

PARSLEY, FLAT-LEAF also known as continental or italian parsley.

POLENTA also known as cornmeal; a flour-like cereal made of dried corn (maize) sold ground in different textures; also the name of the dish that is made from it.

SALSA a chunky sauce served as an accompaniment, often based on tomato, chilli, garlic and onion. May be cooked or uncooked, mild or very spicy.

SWEET PAPRIKA ground, dried red pepper (capsicum). It is available sweet, hot or smoked.

TACO a folded tortilla that has been fried until crisp; tacos are used as a container for spicy meat fillings.

TEQUILA colourless alcoholic liquor of Mexican origin made from the fermented sap of the agave, a desert plant.

TOSTADAS fried tortillas in a stack, with filling in between each tortilla.

TOSTADITAS tortillas torn into pieces and fried; used to scoop up salsa.

VINEGAR
brown malt made from fermented malt and beech shavings.
cider made from fermented apples.
red wine made from red wine.

A

avocado
  chicken and avocado wraps 58
  chilli-seared tuna with avocado cream, tortillas and grilled corn 73
  crab and avocado salad 74
  guacamole 102
  mango and avocado salsa 98

B

banana chillies with potato and green olive stuffing 83
beans
  drunken 96
  grilled lamb with four-bean salad 41
  nachos 12
  salad with tortilla chips 95
  spicy sausages with 29
  tacos, beef and bean 33
  tostadas, bean 24
beef
  burritos 42
  chile con carne 45
  chilli-poached, with fresh corn salsa 26
  chipotle beef tostaditas 8
  fajitas 30
  tacos, beef and bean 33
black bean
  corn and chipotle stew 92
  salsa 101
  soup 19
  spicy chicken with black bean and barley salad 49
blood orange margarita 114
burritos, beef 42

C

caesar salad 84
capsicum
  char-grilled capsicum and green olive salsa 101
  roasted tomato and capsicum soup 20
caramel flans 106
ceviche, lime and ginger 69
chicken
  empanadas, chicken and olive 7
  enchiladas 50
  grilled, with cucumber and tomato salsa 53
  marinated chilli spatchcock 54
  paprika chicken with spicy rice 57
  quesadillas 46
  spicy, with black bean and

barley salad 49
tostadas 53
wings with cherry tomato salsa 61
wraps, chicken and avocado 58
chile con carne 45
chile con queso 24
chilli-poached beef with fresh corn salsa 26
chimichanga with shredded pork, deep-fried 15
chipotle
  beef tostaditas 8
  black bean, corn and chipotle stew 92
  pork ribs with chorizo and smoked paprika 34
  prawns with grilled pineapple, red onion and coriander salad 78
chorizo
  chipotle pork ribs with chorizo and smoked paprika 34
  squid, chorizo and tomato salad 66
  taquitos 11
  warm potato and chorizo salad 87
coconut ice-cream 110
corn
  barbecued, with chunky salsa and mexican rice 80
  black bean, corn and chipotle stew 92
  char-grilled scallops with corn salsa 65
  chickpea corn enchiladas 88
  chilli-poached beef with fresh corn salsa 26
  chilli-seared tuna with avocado cream, tortillas and grilled corn 73
  chunky corn and zucchini salsa 102
  corn and tomato relish 105
  corn and zucchini fritters with avocado salsa 91
  crab, prawn and corn cakes 16
  fish fillets with corn salad 62
  pork and corn wraps 38
crab and avocado salad 74
crab, prawn and corn cakes 16

D

dried fruit compote, rice pudding with 109

E

empanadas, chicken and olive 7

enchiladas
  chicken 50
  chickpea corn 88

F

fajitas 30
fish
  chilli-seared tuna with avocado cream, tortillas and grilled corn 73
  fillets with corn salad 62
  grilled snapper with spicy tomato and lime sauce 70
  lime and ginger ceviche 69

G

guacamole 102

H

hot chocolate 113
huevos rancheros 16

I

ice-cream, coconut 110

L

lamb
  barbecued 37
  grilled, with four-bean salad 41
lime
  and mint cooler 113
  ceviche, lime and ginger 69
  tortilla lime soup 8

M

mango and avocado salsa 98
mango cheeks, grilled 110
margarita
  blood orange 114
  chilli 115
  classic 114

N

nachos, bean 12

O

olives
  banana chillies with potato and green olive stuffing 83
  chicken and olive empanadas 7
  roasted capsicum and green olive salsa 101

P

polenta carnitas with salsa cruda 23
pork
  chipotle pork ribs with chorizo and paprika 34
  deep-fried chimichanga with shredded pork 15
  pork and cheese quesadillas 4
  pork and corn tortilla wraps 38
potato
  banana chillies with potato and green olive stuffing 83

potato and chorizo salad 87
prawns
  chipotle prawns with grilled pineapple, red onion and coriander salad 78
  crab, prawn and corn cakes 16
  slow-cooked spicy garlic prawns 77

Q

quesadillas
  chicken 46
  pork and cheese 4

R

rice
  barbecued, with chunky salsa and mexican rice 80
  paprika chicken with spicy rice 57
  pudding with dried fruit compote 109

S

salsa
  avocado 91
  black bean 101
  char-grilled capsicum and green olive 101
  chunky corn and zucchini 102
  chunky tomato 11
  cruda 23, 30
  mango and avocado 98
  verde 98
sangria mexicana 115
scallops with corn salsa, char-grilled 65
spatchcock, marinated chilli 54
squid, chorizo and tomato salad 66
sweet potato, chilli-glazed 88

T

tacos, beef and bean 33
taquitos, chorizo 11
tomato
  bean and tomato tostadas 24
  chunky tomato salsa 11
  corn and tomato relish 105
  roasted tomato and capsicum soup 20
  squid, chorizo and tomato salad 66
  tomato, chilli and raisin relish 105
tortilla lime soup 8
tostadas
  bean and tomato 24
  chicken 53
tostaditas, chipotle beef 8

W

wedding cookies 109

Z

zucchini
  corn and zucchini salsa 102
  corn and zucchini fritters with avocado salsa 91

INDEX

MEASURES

One Australian metric measuring cup holds approximately 250ml; one Australian metric tablespoon holds 20ml; one Australian metric teaspoon holds 5ml.

The difference between one country's measuring cups and another's is within a two- or three-teaspoon variance, and will not affect your cooking results. North America, New Zealand and the United Kingdom use a 15ml tablespoon.

All cup and spoon measurements are level. The most accurate way of measuring dry ingredients is to weigh them. When measuring liquids, use a clear glass or plastic jug with the metric markings.

We use large eggs with an average weight of 60g.

DRY MEASURES

METRIC	IMPERIAL
15g	½oz
30g	1oz
60g	2oz
90g	3oz
125g	4oz (¼lb)
155g	5oz
185g	6oz
220g	7oz
250g	8oz (½lb)
280g	9oz
315g	10oz
345g	11oz
375g	12oz (¾lb)
410g	13oz
440g	14oz
470g	15oz
500g	16oz (1lb)
750g	24oz (1½lb)
1kg	32oz (2lb)

LIQUID MEASURES

METRIC	IMPERIAL
30ml	1 fluid oz
60ml	2 fluid oz
100ml	3 fluid oz
125ml	4 fluid oz
150ml	5 fluid oz (¼ pint/1 gill)
190ml	6 fluid oz
250ml	8 fluid oz
300ml	10 fluid oz (½ pint)
500ml	16 fluid oz
600ml	20 fluid oz (1 pint)
1000ml (1 litre)	1¾ pints

LENGTH MEASURES

METRIC	IMPERIAL
3mm	⅛in
6mm	¼in
1cm	½in
2cm	¾in
2.5cm	1in
5cm	2in
6cm	2½in
8cm	3in
10cm	4in
13cm	5in
15cm	6in
18cm	7in
20cm	8in
23cm	9in
25cm	10in
28cm	11in
30cm	12in (1ft)

OVEN TEMPERATURES

These oven temperatures are only a guide for conventional ovens.
For fan-forced ovens, check the manufacturer's manual.

	°C (CELSIUS)	°F (FAHRENHEIT)	GAS MARK
Very slow	120	250	½
Slow	150	275-300	1-2
Moderately slow	160	325	3
Moderate	180	350-375	4-5
Moderately hot	200	400	6
Hot	220	425-450	7-8
Very hot	240	475	9

CONVERSION CHART

ARE YOU MISSING SOME OF THE WORLD'S FAVOURITE COOKBOOKS?

The Australian Women's Weekly Cookbooks are available from bookshops, cookshops, supermarkets and other stores all over the world. You can also buy direct from the publisher, using the order form below.

TITLE	RRP	QTY	TITLE	RRP	QTY
Asian, Meals in Minutes	£6.99		Japanese Cooking Class	£6.99	
Babies & Toddlers Good Food	£6.99		Kids' Birthday Cakes	£6.99	
Barbecue Meals In Minutes	£6.99		Kids Cooking	£6.99	
Beginners Cooking Class	£6.99		Lean Food	£6.99	
Beginners Simple Meals	£6.99		Low-carb, Low-fat	£6.99	
Beginners Thai	£6.99		Low-fat Feasts	£6.99	
Best Food	£6.99		Low-fat Food For Life	£6.99	
Best Food Desserts	£6.99		Low-fat Meals in Minutes	£6.99	
Best Food Fast	£6.99		Main Course Salads	£6.99	
Best Food Mains	£6.99		Mexican	£6.99	
Cakes Biscuits & Slices	£6.99		Middle Eastern Cooking Class	£6.99	
Cakes Cooking Class	£6.99		Midweek Meals in Minutes	£6.99	
Caribbean Cooking	£6.99		Muffins, Scones & Breads	£6.99	
Casseroles	£6.99		New Casseroles	£6.99	
Chicken	£6.99		New Classics	£6.99	
Chicken Meals in Minutes	£6.99		New Finger Food	£6.99	
Chinese Cooking Class	£6.99		New Salads (Oct 06)	£6.99	
Christmas Cooking	£6.99		Party Food and Drink	£6.99	
Chocolate	£6.99		Pasta Meals in Minutes	£6.99	
Cocktails	£6.99		Potatoes	£6.99	
Cooking for Friends	£6.99		Salads: Simple, Fast & Fresh	£6.99	
Detox	£6.99		Saucery	£6.99	
Dinner Beef	£6.99		Sauces Salsas & Dressings	£6.99	
Dinner Lamb	£6.99		Sensational Stir-Fries	£6.99	
Dinner Seafood	£6.99		Short-order Cook	£6.99	
Easy Australian Style	£6.99		Slim	£6.99	
Easy Curry	£6.99		Stir-fry	£6.99	
Easy Spanish-Style	£6.99		Superfoods for Exam Success	£6.99	
Essential Soup	£6.99		Sweet Old Fashioned Favourites	£6.99	
French Food, New	£6.99		Tapas Mezze Antipasto & other bites	£6.99	
Fresh Food for Babies & Toddlers	£6.99		Thai Cooking Class	£6.99	
Get Real, Make a Meal	£6.99		Traditional Italian	£6.99	
Good Food Fast	£6.99		Vegetarian Meals in Minutes	£6.99	
Great Lamb Cookbook	£6.99		Vegie Food	£6.99	
Greek Cooking Class	£6.99		Weekend Cook	£6.99	
Grills	£6.99		Wicked Sweet Indulgences	£6.99	
Healthy Heart Cookbook	£6.99		Wok, Meals in Minutes	£6.99	
Indian Cooking Class	£6.99		TOTAL COST:	£	

Mr/Mrs/Ms _____

Address _____

_____ Postcode _____

Day time phone _____ Email* (optional) _____

I enclose my cheque/money order for £ _____

or please charge £ _____

to my: ☐ Access ☐ Mastercard ☐ Visa ☐ Diners Club

PLEASE NOTE: WE DO NOT ACCEPT SWITCH OR ELECTRON CARDS

Card number ☐☐☐☐ ☐☐☐☐ ☐☐☐☐ ☐☐☐☐

Expiry date _____ 3 digit security code *(found on reverse of card)* _____

Cardholder's name_____ Signature _____

To order: Mail or fax – photocopy or complete the order form above, and send your credit card details or cheque payable to: Australian Consolidated Press (UK), Moulton Park Business Centre, Red House Road, Moulton Park, Northampton NN3 6AQ, phone (+44) (0) 1604 497531 fax (+44) (0) 1604 497533, e-mail books@acpmedia.co.uk or order online at www.acpuk.com

Non-UK residents: We accept the credit cards listed on the coupon, or cheques, drafts or International Money Orders payable in sterling and drawn on a UK bank. Credit card charges are at the exchange rate current at the time of payment.

Postage and packing UK: Add £1.00 per order plus 50p per book.

Postage and packing overseas: Add £2.00 per order plus £1.00 per book.

All pricing current at time of going to press and subject to change/availability.

Offer ends 31.12.2007

* By including your email address, you consent to receipt of any email regarding this magazine, and other emails which inform you of ACP's other publications, products, services and events, and to promote third party goods and services you may be interested in.